Colchester 24

Andrew Phillips
& Anthony Cody

AMBERLEY PUBLISHING

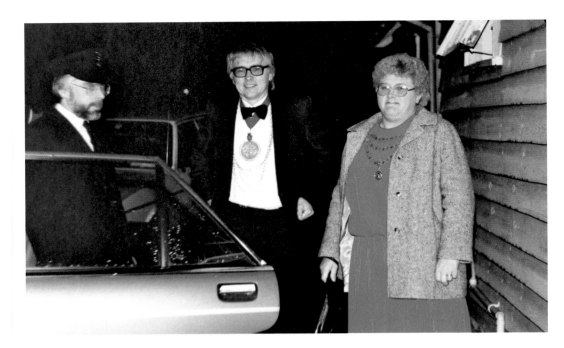

21 October 1986
Mayor Bob Russell and his wife Audrey arrive in the mayoral car at the former Officers' Club, now destroyed by fire. *Photograph:* Chris Elliott.

To all the photographers of Colchester 24.

First published 2012

Amberley Publishing
The Hill, Stroud
Gloucestershire, GL5 4EP

www.amberley-books.com

Copyright © Andrew Phillips & Anthony Cody, 2012

The right of Andrew Phillips & Anthony Cody
to be identified as the Authors of this work
has been asserted in accordance with the
Copyrights, Designs and Patents Act 1988.

ISBN 978 1 4456 1056 6

British Library Cataloguing in Publication Data.
A catalogue record for this book is available from
the British Library.

Typeset in 9.5pt on 12pt Celeste.
Typesetting by Amberley Publishing.
Printed in the UK.

Introduction

When I was Mayor of Colchester in 1986 it was my pleasure to open an exhibition of local photography called 'Just Another Day', in which twenty local photographers had combined to capture life in Colchester over a 24-hour period on October 21 and 22 that year. Twenty-five years passed, and in 2011 another team of photographers founded the Colchester 24 Trust to photograph Colchester over another 24-hour period from noon on Friday 21 October to noon on Saturday 22 October 2011 – just twenty-five years after the original event.

By now, of course, there had been a revolution in photography thanks to the widespread availability of electronic cameras. *Colchester 24* was thrown open to the public, inviting them to capture life in Colchester in 2011. The outcome was overwhelming. Over 5,000 electronic photos were contributed (including several taken by myself) by almost 200 photographers. Chance meant that I featured in both sets of photos – though I had grown older in the process!

I therefore hope you will be as enthralled as I have been to see in this book some of the best of those photographs, telling the story of Colchester today.

Sir Bob Russell
MP for Colchester

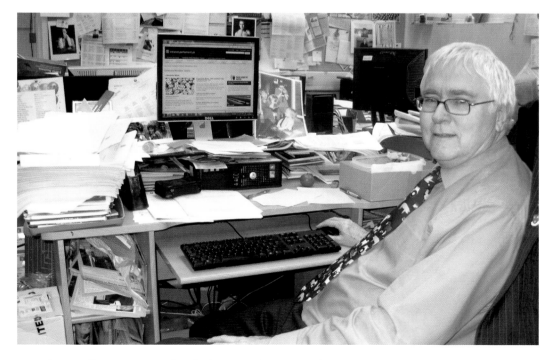

Sir Bob Russell MP, sitting at his desk, 21 October 2011. *Photograph:* Simon Hunkin.

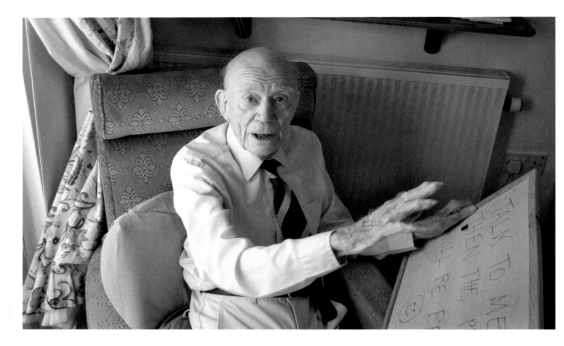

1986–2011

In 1986 George Royffe, aged seventy-five, befriended the 'punks' who sat on the walls of Holy Trinity Church, outside the Cups pub. Result: a memorable photo, frozen in time (*below*). In 2011 (*above*), George Royffe, aged 100, was 'patron' of *Colchester 24*, a repeat project, inviting the public to record the social history of Colchester in one 24-hour period. *Photographs*: Alan Murrells, George Royffe.

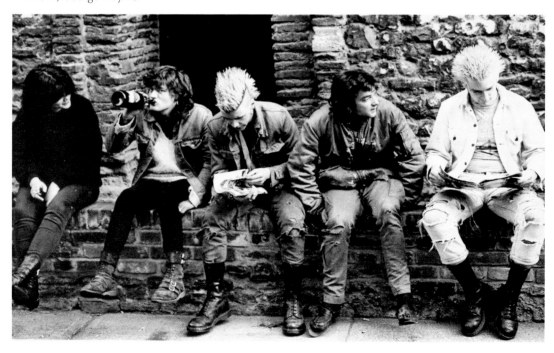

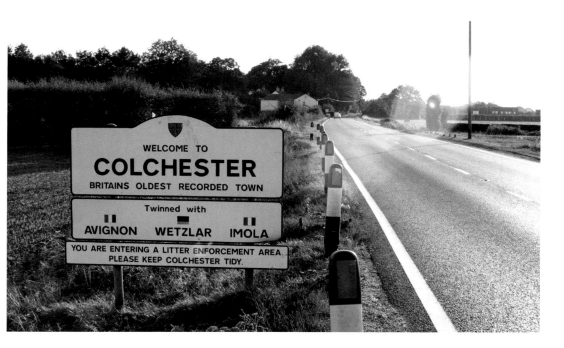

What is Colchester?

It is 'Britain's Oldest Recorded Town' – every approach road says so. And, standing on a hill, surrounded by a wall the Romans built, it has been a historic town for 2,000 years. Today the wall survives in many places. Buildings stand on it (*below*), and Colchester streets have historic structures from every age. This fuels a tension between progress and conservation; whether to give developers their head and knock down old buildings, or whether to find them a new use. Colchester has done both. *Photographs*: Bob Finch, Steve Robinson.

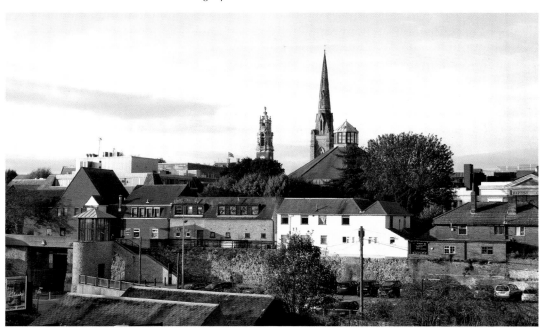

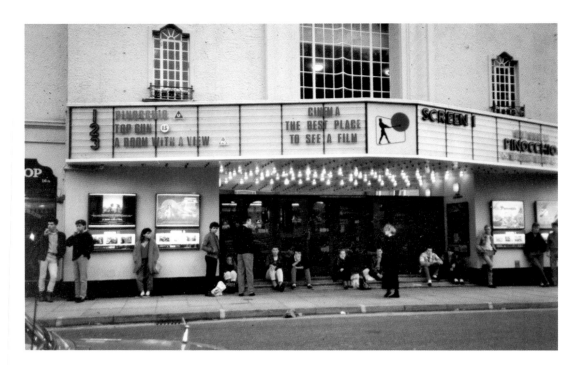

Then & Now

Colchester 24 was inspired by its 1986 predecessor, but no effort was made to take the same photos in 2011. Nor can this book carry many 1986 photos. However, occasionally we caught change taking place. Colchester's 'historic' Odeon Cinema (*above*) still had customers in 1986. By 2011 (*below*) it was an empty shell. Refused planning permission to become a nightclub, it sits gaunt and vulnerable, its Wurlitzer organ long gone, perhaps facing demolition. *Photographs*: Carol Murrells, Ricky Kinzett.

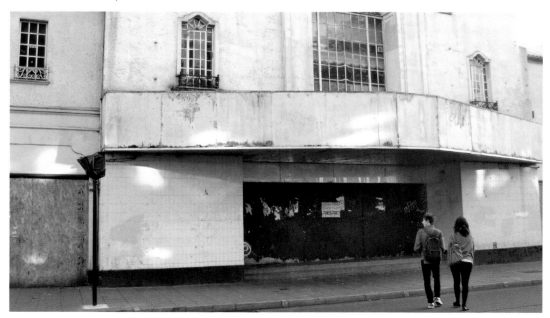

ROUTES

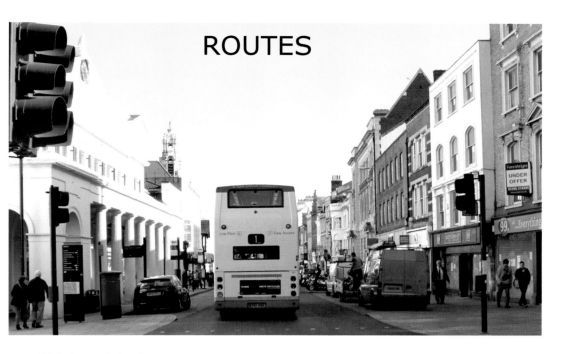

High Street Splendour

Colchester's broad High Street deserves respect. It was the main street of the first city in Britain. Romans shopped here. From the fire office to the castle, it is our showplace street and a Conservation Area. The council has protected the long line of period buildings on the shadowed side of the street, even though, in a few places, only the façades survive, and steel and concrete props up the retail therapy within. *Photographs*: Charlotte Hinchliffe, Richard Lyon.

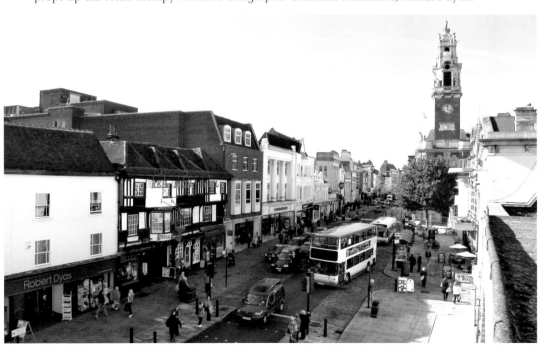

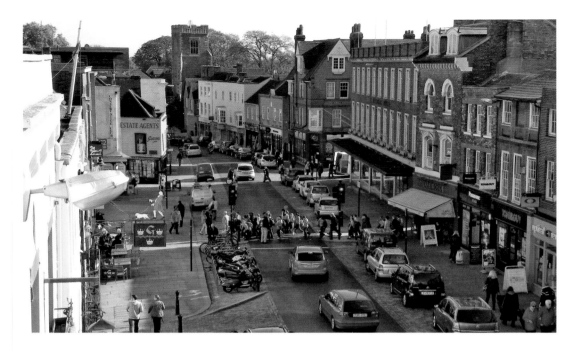

High Street Traffic

In 1986 High Street had two lanes of one-way traffic. Now, by creating a single line of traffic, the council has reduced speed levels, facilitated emergency parking, preserved the taxi rank, planted a lot of bollards, and built bicycle racks (*below*). Our rooftop view (*above*), looking down High Street, shows today's traffic/pedestrian interface working well; but plans now exist to restrict High Street for most of the day to buses, taxis and bicycles. *Photographs*: Richard Lyon, Laurence Tobin.

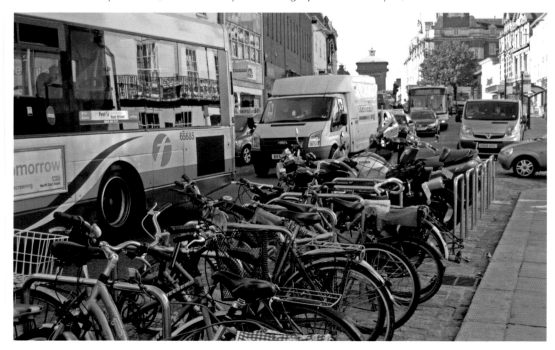

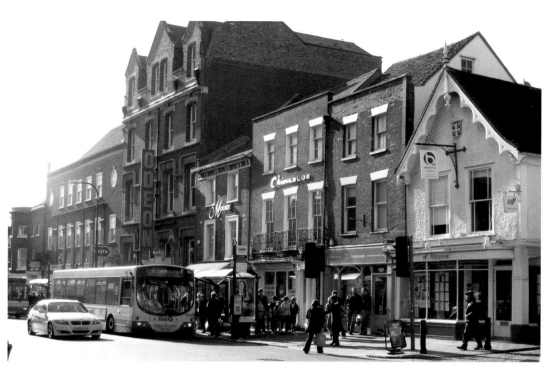

Head Street

Head Street originally linked two gates in our Roman wall. Today (*above*) it is dominated on one side by the new Odeon Cinema. This building began life as the town's Victorian post office, built high to house the business created by the Penny Post. Note the successful conversion of an historic building, retaining its façade while providing a modern cinema in the unseen space behind. The younger age group (*below*) provides many of the customers. *Photographs*: Andrew Phillips.

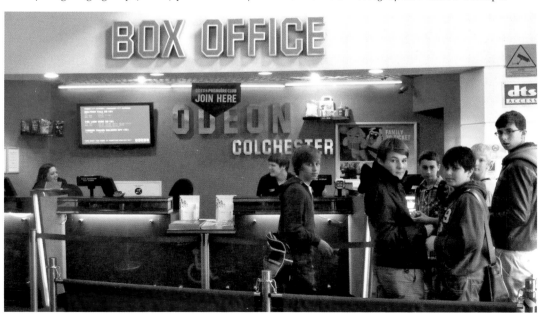

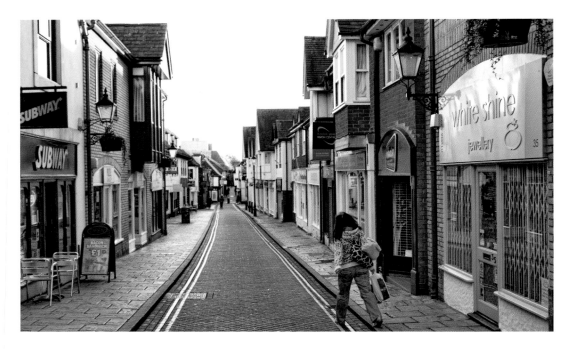

Eld Lane (once Old Lane)

(*Above*) Caught in the early morning, Sir Isaac's Walk and Eld Lane, built on the Roman Wall, resemble one long narrow street of old shops. In fact the buildings are mostly modern, built to mirror the traditional historic town. (*Below*) Hours later Eld Lane is alive with people, its kaleidoscope of small shops part of Colchester's rich shopping experience. *Photographs*: Roy Essery, John Soliven.

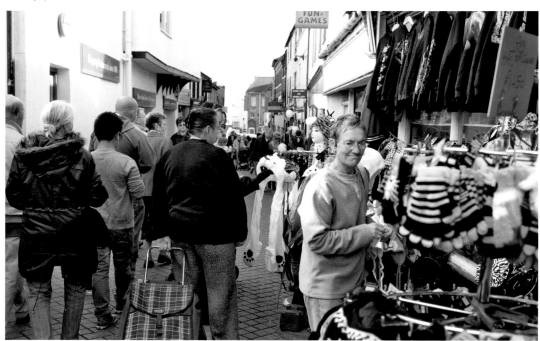

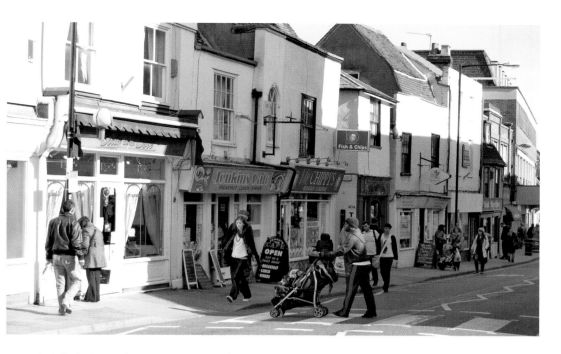

St John's Street (once Gutter Street)

Parallel to Eld Lane, St John's Street belongs to 'historic' Colchester. The sunny side of the street (*above*) is full of traditional buildings, but a shadow is cast on them by the large Greek portico opposite (*below*). This was pasted onto a supermarket built in 1986 for Tesco, who soon left. Since then the building has been broken up into several units, which now showcase the most interesting bus stops in Colchester. *Photographs*: Tina Cave, Joe Sales.

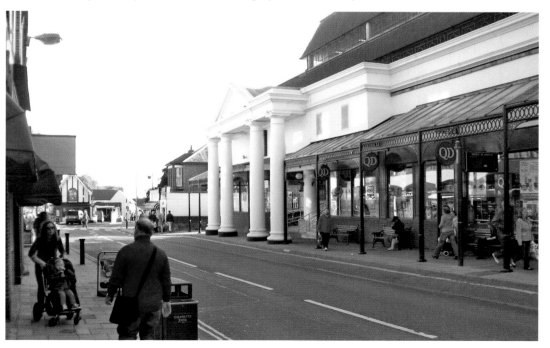

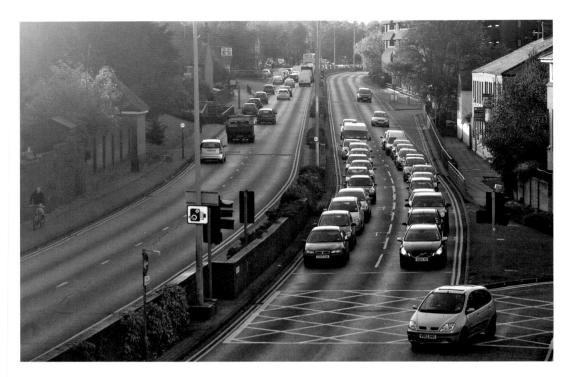

Cars & Car Parks

Parallel to St John's Street is Southway (*above*), part of Colchester's unfinished inner ring road. It joins Balkerne Hill (*see* book cover) and Westway to form two sides of an oblong. There matters stopped. Over the years an extension of Southway and the widening of Cowdray Avenue have been promised, discussed and postponed. Since 1970 car numbers have doubled. Cars need car parks (*below*) and our ring roads access four multi-storeys. *Photographs*: Steve Robinson, Mark Cave.

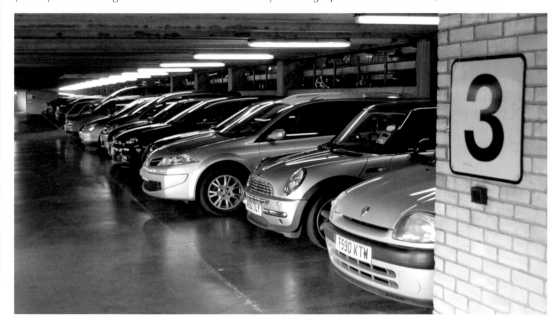

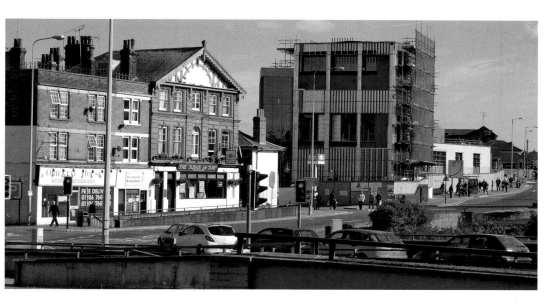

St Botolph's

(*Above*) Southway stops at St Botolph's Roundabout. Here sit Colchester's new Magistrates' Courts, still under construction during *Colchester 24*. The Victorian pub beside it has been optimistically renamed the Judge & the Jury. (*Below*) Living over the shop was once common. Hence our many large Victorian shops where the Victorian ground floor has gone, leaving three 'domestic' storeys above and three shops below: an oriental supermarket, a 'Gentleman's Club' and a noodle bar. *Photographs*: Tina Cave, Andrew Phillips.

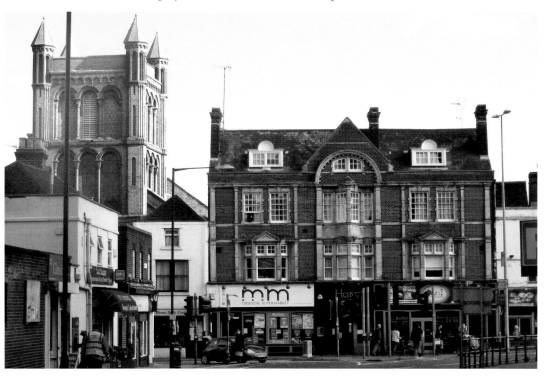

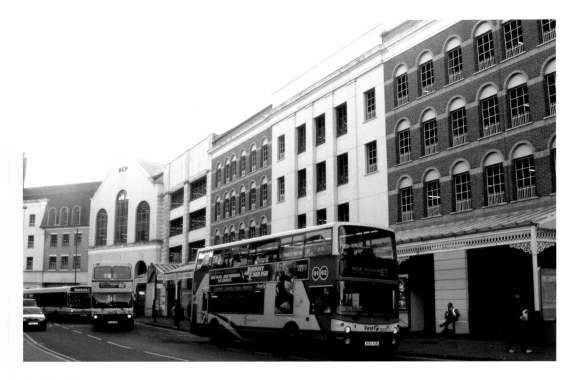

Bus Stations

Round the corner from Southway lies Osborne Street car park (*above*) in all its splendour. That Legoland architecture is to hide the brutal concrete with which multi-storey car parks are built. Osborne Street will house Colchester's new bus station, following the controversial closure of the present one, now overshadowed by Colchester's new Firstsite gallery. (*Below*) Two worlds in conflict as a battalion of First buses make a last stand below Firstsite's golden walls. *Photographs*: Andrew Phillips.

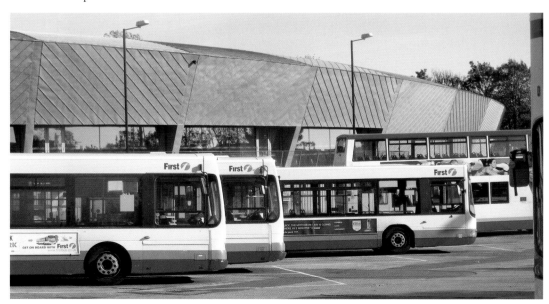

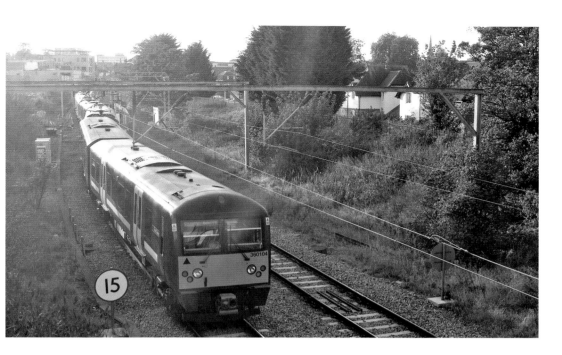

Railway Stations

The Victorians left us three train stations: North station, on the main line from London; Hythe station, built to start a line to Clacton; and Colchester Town, built by the Hawkins brothers, who owned timber yards at the Hythe. (*Above*) A train rumbles out of Colchester Town. (*Below*) Notice the shadow across this photograph of the new railway bridge at North station. This has facilitated Colchester's most complex road junction, as land beyond the bridge is developed. *Photographs*: Steve Robinson, Mark Cave.

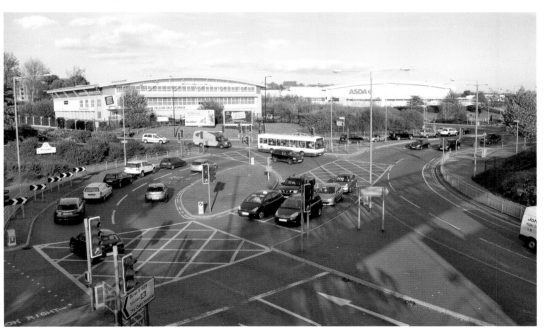

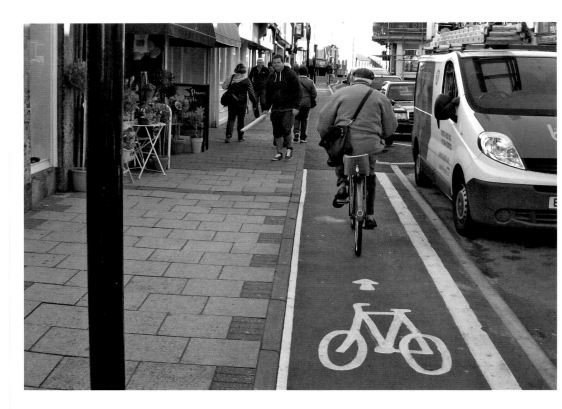

Cycleways

Between 2008 and 2011 Colchester was awarded £4.2 million to encourage travel by bike and develop cycleways, but town centre streets have not easily adapted. (*Above*) The cycleway in Crouch Street is notoriously hazardous, crossing the road twice and encroaching on pavement space. Down on Hythe Quay (*below*) this cycleway weaves off the main road and over Colne Causeway to the opposite shore where it runs the 2-mile Wivenhoe Trail. *Photographs*: Joe Sales, Rodney Woods.

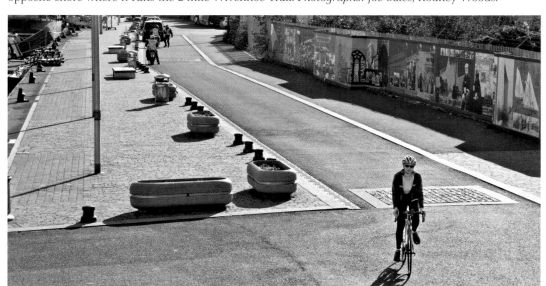

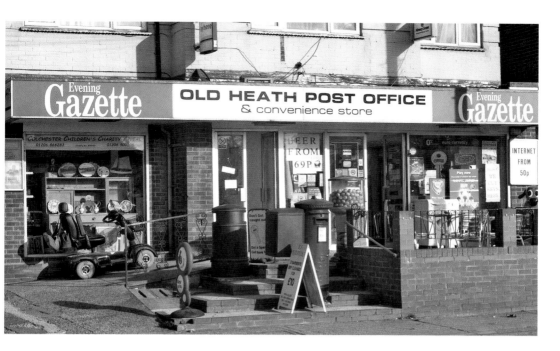

The Suburbs

Beyond central Colchester vast suburbs ring the town. Community facilities can be a problem. Post offices and general stores like this one at Old Heath (*above*) are under threat from waves of recent closures and a growth of out-of-town supermarkets. The Greenstead Community Centre (*below*), opened in 2003 in one of Colchester's largest mass housing areas, is the focus of much community activity. *Photographs*: Steve Robinson, Rebecca Sayer.

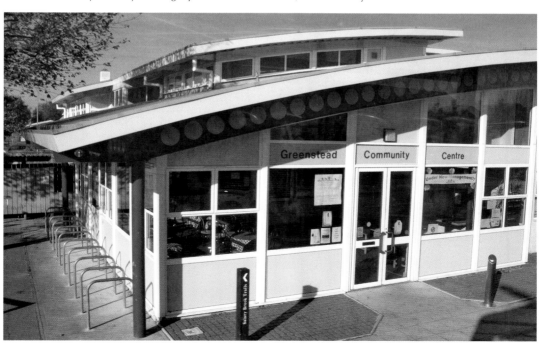

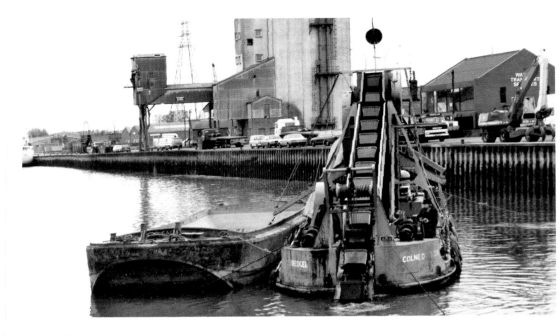

The Hythe: Decay

(*Above*) In 1986 Colchester's Hythe, 1¼ miles from the town centre, was still a registered port, a position it had held for 900 years. This antique bucket dredger still scooped out mud to keep the channel deep enough for large ships to dock. Beyond, stands the King Edward Quay and the towering Hasler grain elevator, which is now gone. By 2011 (*below*) the port was closed and, near the road bridge, evidence of picturesque decay abounds: a dead barge, empty Victorian warehouses and a channel now clogged with mud. *Photographs*: Simon Banks, Sandra Woods.

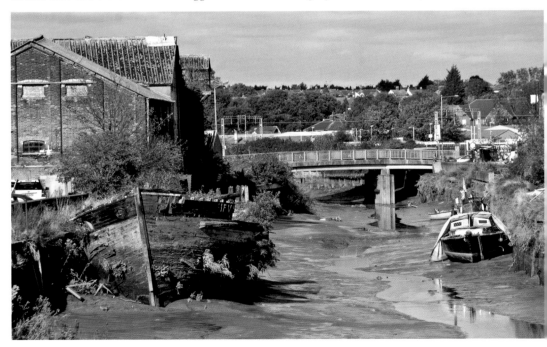

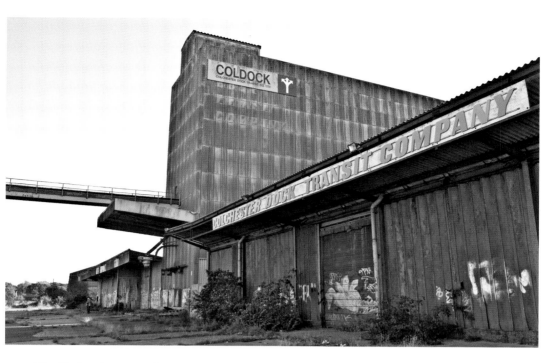

The Hythe: Regeneration

Down river (*above*) the massive 'Coldock' warehouses of the late Colchester Dock Transit Co. lie prey to rust, rats and graffiti, while upriver (*below*) a new Hythe 'district' is bursting into life. Its basis is small unit housing – high rise flats, student accommodation, warehouses and superstores. River 'colour' is provided by a handful of lived-in barges and the sea cadets' newly-painted lightship, which once stood off the Kent Coast. *Photographs*: Rodney Woods.

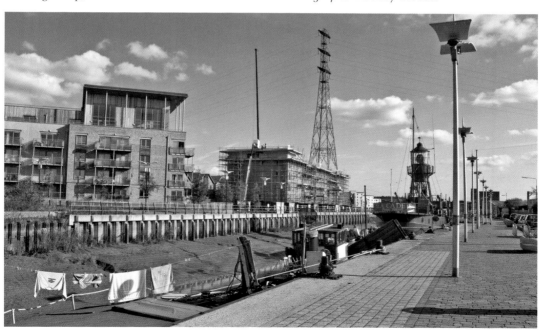

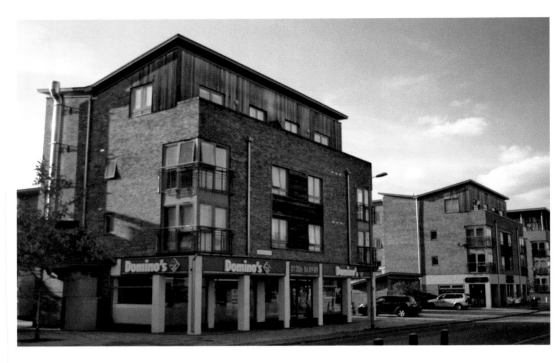

The Hythe: Accommodation

In 2011 the focus of new building was on the east side of the Hythe. (*Above*) Domino's Pizza in Lightship Way stands strategically among blocks of new housing in the shadow of a giant B&Q warehouse. (*Below*) A family group hangs out below the windows of University Quays, the high-rise student accommodation built in recent years. *Photographs*: Simona Szakacs.

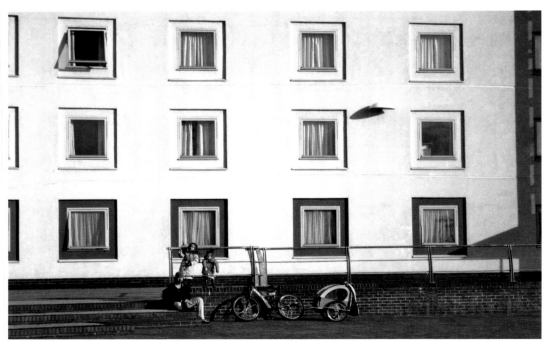

FORCES

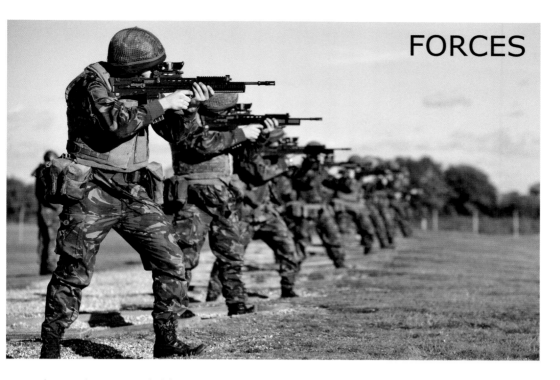

The Garrison at Work (1)

Colchester is a major garrison town. The relocation of the Army to new accommodation in Merville Barracks has opened up large areas of Army land for redevelopment. (*Above*) Members of the Parachute Regiment at weapons practice on the Middlewick Ranges. The regular Friday workout for members of the Royal Logistics is shown below. *Photographs*: Sgt Rupert Frere.

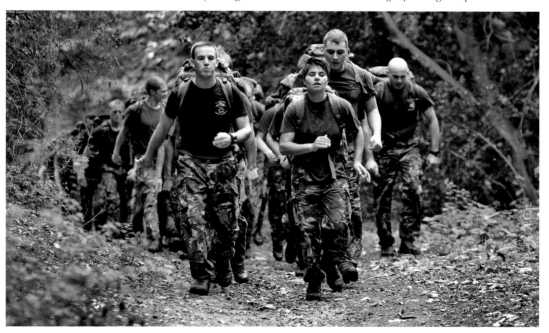

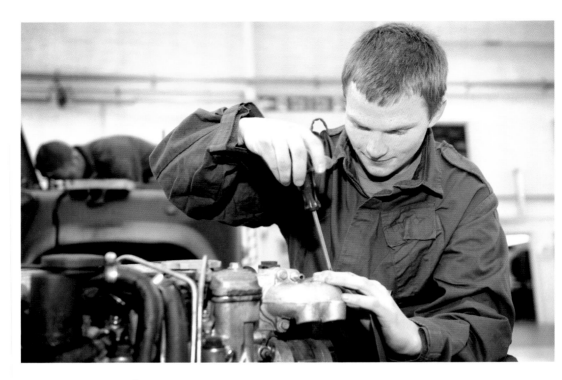

The Garrison at Work (2)

(*Above*) A member of the Royal Electrical Mechanical Engineers busy on Land Rover maintenance in Merville Barracks. (*Below*) No, not a breakdown – members of the Medical Regiment push a driver and Land Rover backwards round the parade ground at the double as part of their Battle Physical Training. *Photographs:* Sgt Rupert Frere.

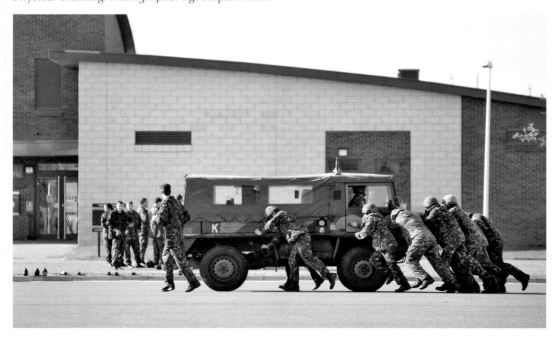

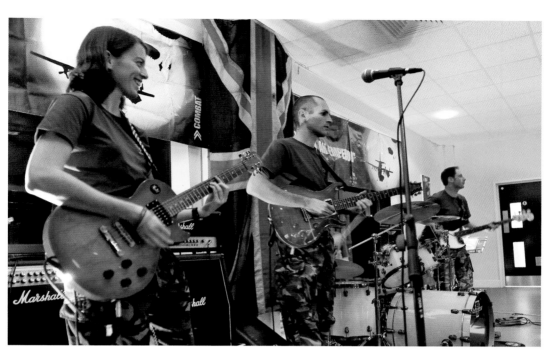

The Garrison at Play
(*Above*) The Parachute Regiment band plays for a Charity Event in the Army Gymnasium. (*Below*) Married quarters are home for Leanne and Billy with their dog, Cory. There are over 1,000 Services' Family Houses in Colchester. *Photographs*: Sgt Rupert Frere.

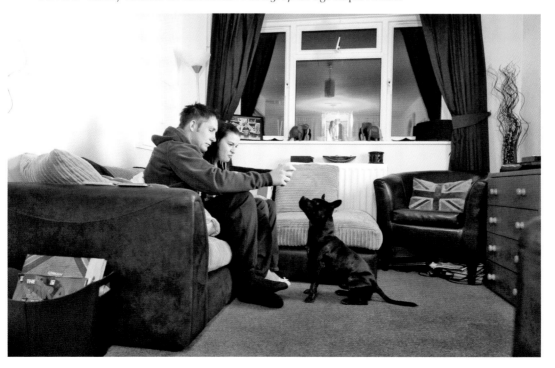

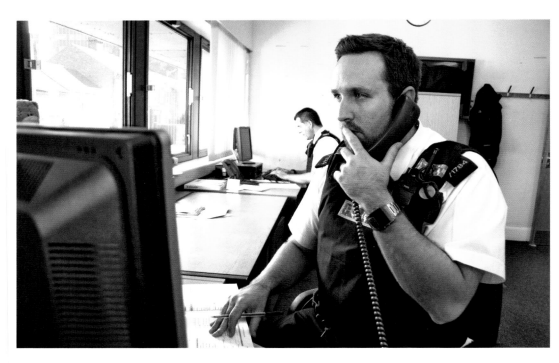

Police (1)

There are over 300 police officers based in Colchester. (*Above*) In Colchester Police Station, prior to going on shift, two police officers follow up enquiries from their previous shift. (*Below*) Two Police Community Security Officers on foot patrol deal with an enquiry in Eld Lane. *Photographs*: David White.

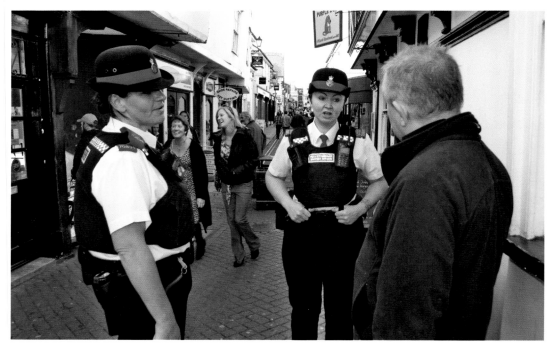

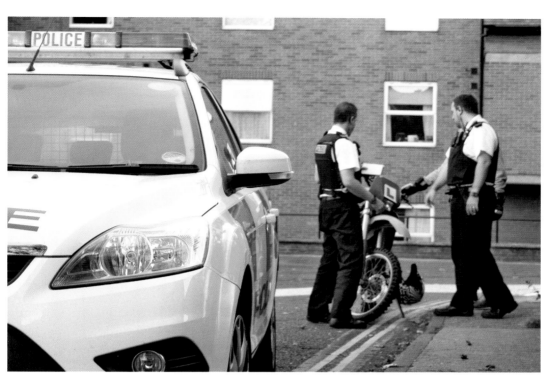

Police (2)

Patrol cars do shifts of eight to eleven hours. Above, a learner motorcyclist caught speeding along Head Street is questioned just inside Balkerne Gardens about his driving behaviour and subsequently (*below*) is given a fixed penalty ticket. *Photographs*: David White.

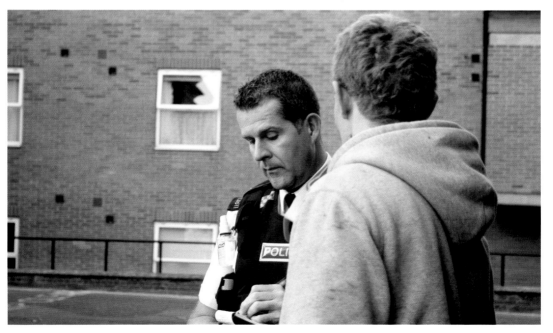

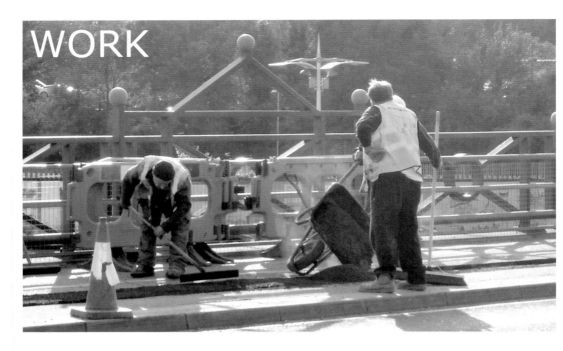

WORK

Manual

Manual work is a declining form of employment, but, kitted in yellow hi-vis jackets, such men are still a familiar sight. (*Above*) On Colne Causeway three workers lay tarmac following cable-laying across the bridge. (*Below*) Steve of the Borough Recycling and Waste Service loads plastic waste into the Borough's purpose-built vehicle. *Photographs*: Jules Linton, Andrew Phillips.

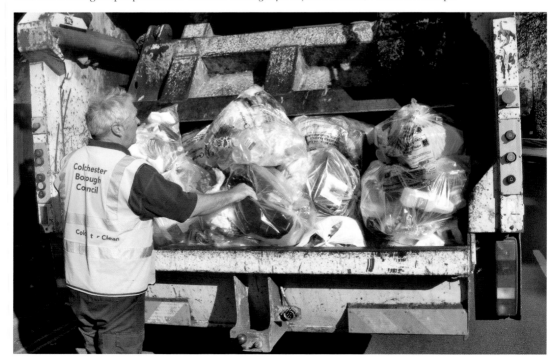

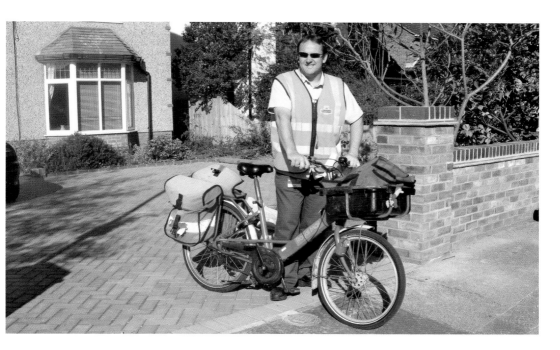

Services

Equipped with his bike and his panniers, the 'postie' is a universal Colchester figure. After four years working the same patch, Alan (*above*) knows it well. Greater Colchester is served by almost 1,000 postmen. (*Below*) In Stanwell Street three BT officials check the Wi-Fi signal at a street cabinet. The man on the left is not phoning a friend but probably checking the signal has reached the Exchange. *Photographs*: Andrew Phillips, Dave Clarke.

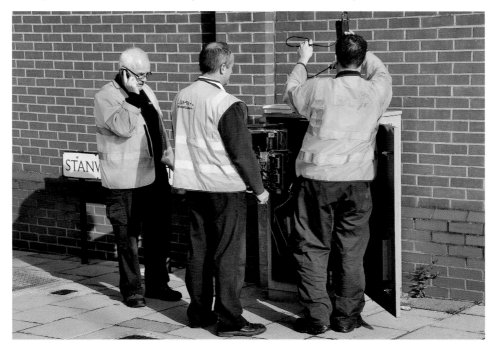

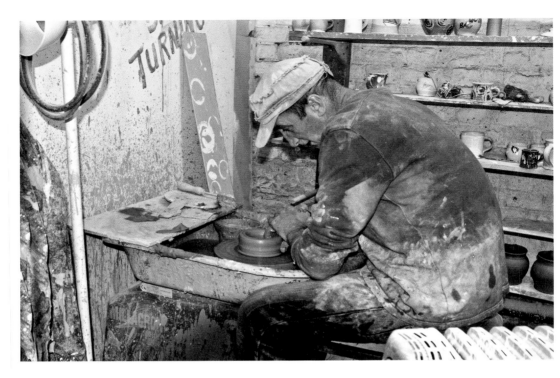

Craftsmanship

(*Above*) David the potter begins to throw a mug in his workshop down at the Hythe. (*Below*) Another David is completing a new unit for Pine Valley Interiors at their workshop in Gosbecks Road. *Photographs*: Sandra Woods, Ivan Beales.

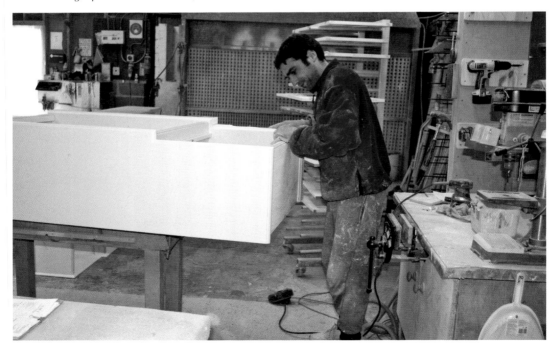

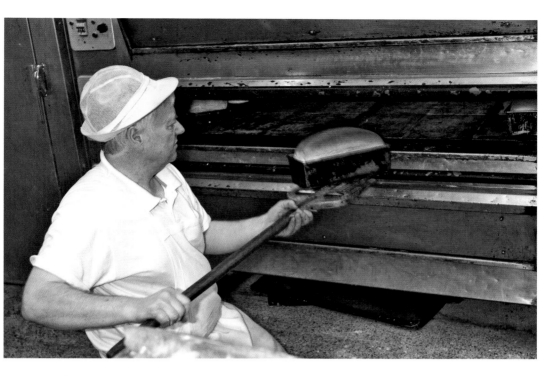

Catering

(*Above*) Roger Hanse, the last independent family baker in Colchester, tests the day's first batch of loaves, all made by traditional methods. (*Below*) After decades of decline, fish and chip shops are recovering. Inside John's Fish Bar Michael throws another basket of chips into the pan. *Photographs*: David Robinson, Ivan Beales.

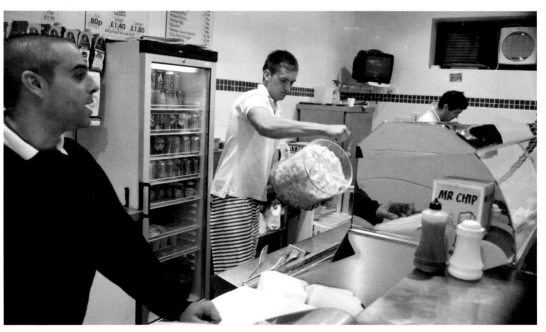

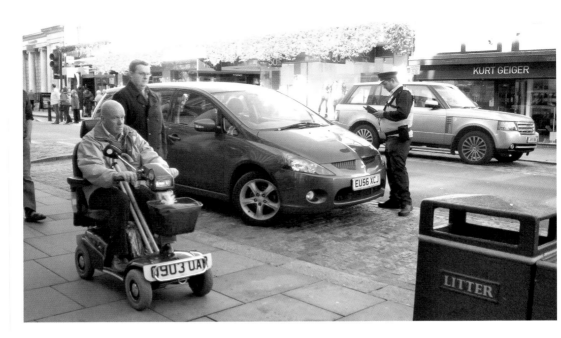

Mobility

(*Above*) Using his hand held computer, a Borough Enforcement Officer checks High Street parking, while a mobility scooter manoeuvres past a litter bin. (*Below*) Colchester is slowly becoming more wheelchair-friendly. Big Issue sellers like Charlie are now familiar figures. Though sales can be very slow, the licensed sellers retain a patient stoicism. *Photographs*: Kath Tobin, John Pollard.

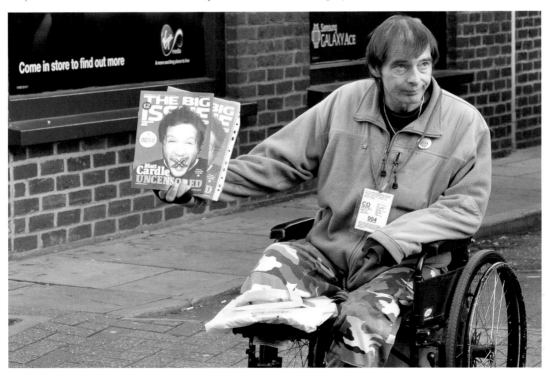

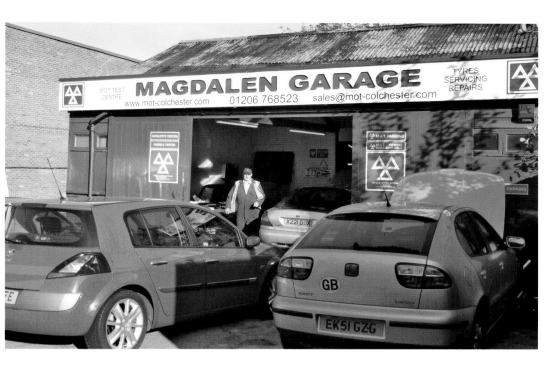

Mechanics

Small garages are still found in Colchester, even though car maintenance is increasingly high-tech. Above, the Magdalen Street Garage advertises tyres, servicing, repairs and MOT test facilities. (*Below*) Friday evening at the neighbourhood West Lodge Garage: mopping out done, it's time to go home. *Photographs*: Delia Brooks, Andrew Phillips.

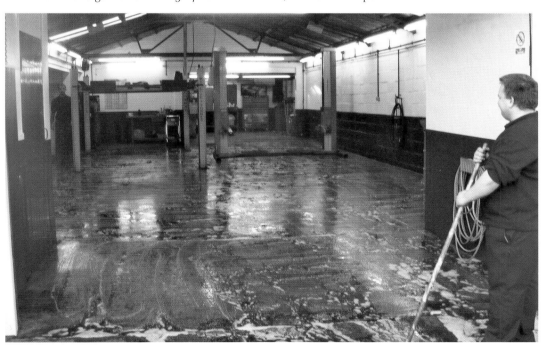

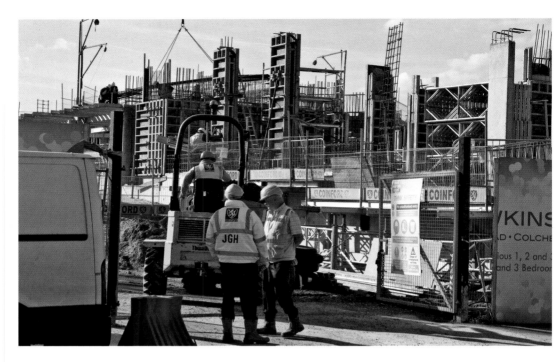

Construction (1)

In 2011 Colchester was declared 'the fastest growing town in Britain'. Many felt this was unwelcome news and was because too many flats had been built. (*Above*) Hawkins Warf is a major development on the east bank of the Hythe. (*Below*) The completion of detailed paperwork accompanies the building of Colchester's new landmark Magistrates' Court at St Botolph's Corner. *Photographs*: Rodney Woods, Mark Whiting.

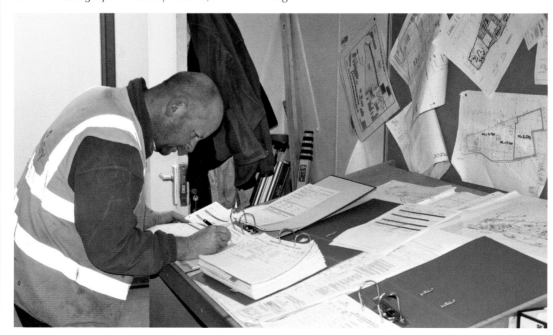

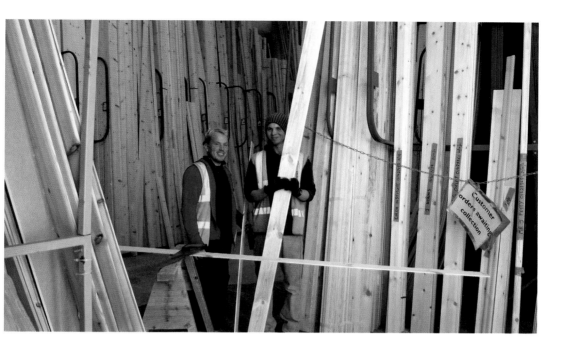

Construction (2)

Long-established building merchants KB (Kent, Blaxill) cater for both wholesale and DIY customers. (*Above*) Tom and Philip guard the timber section, which contains 'customer orders awaiting collection'. (*Below*) KB has long been noted for their expertise in glass. Lee works on the computer-controlled cutting table capable of cutting glass from multi-paned piles. It can also cut definable shapes from scanned templates. It cannot yet fry eggs. *Photographs*: Sandra Hartley.

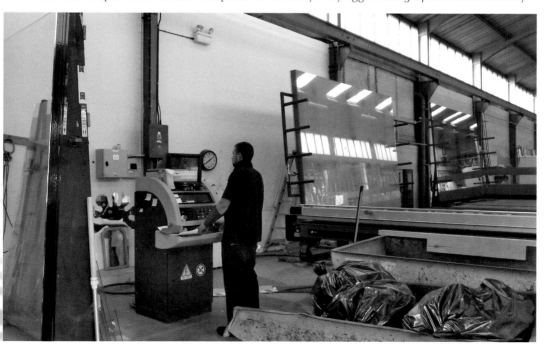

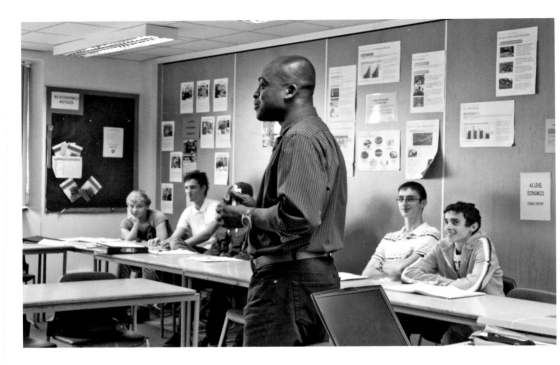

Preparation

(*Above*) Mr Tahoulan, teaching Economics at the Sixth Form College, seems to have client attention as he prepares his students for their A level exam. (*Below*) Denise makes poached eggs in the kitchen of the Cameo Café, haunt of Mercury Theatre actors. *Photographs*: Christine Alexander, Alan Murrells.

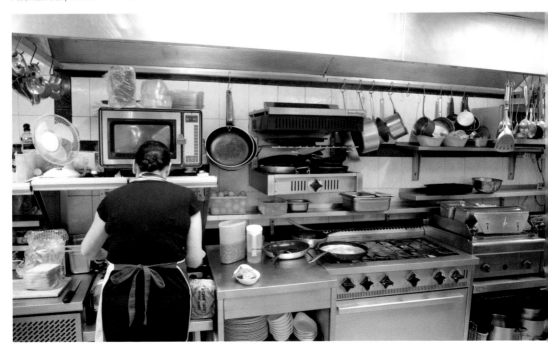

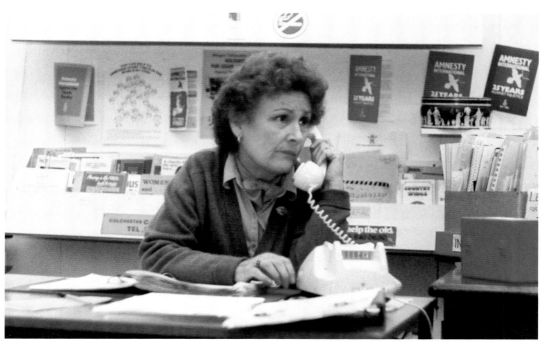

Communication
The modern switchboard facilitates both call centres and intensive operations for large institutions. Contrast the 1986 photograph of Mary Leonard, (*above*) fielding calls in the Colchester Community Service Office, with that of Ann Richell (*below*) at her work station in the Customer Service section of Essex County Council in Severalls Business Park. The unit handles an average of 3,000 calls a day. *Photographs*: Chris Elliott, Chris Simmonds.

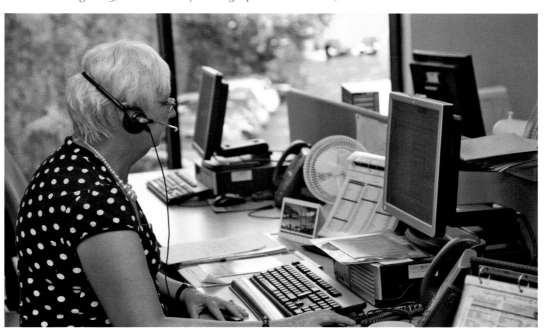

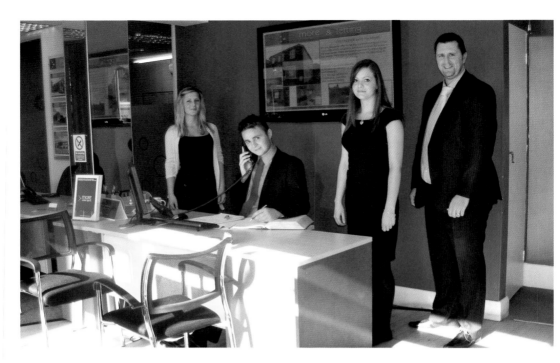

White Collars

White collar work occupies most of us. (*Above*) Staff of More Estate Agent's kindly pose for the camera. Since this photograph was taken they have moved premises and quadrupled their workspace. (*Below*) Dr Gordon Coutts, Chief Executive of the Colchester Hospital University NHS Trust, keeps a clean modern desk, his modest in-tray belying considerable responsibilities. *Photographs*: Andrew Phillips, Martin Gould.

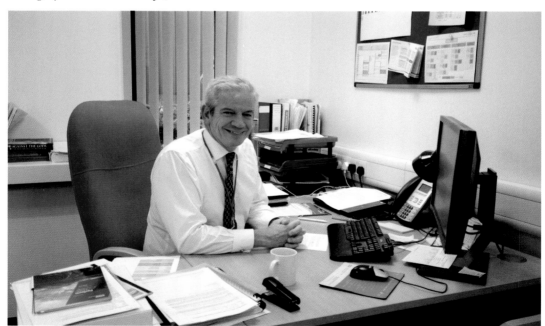

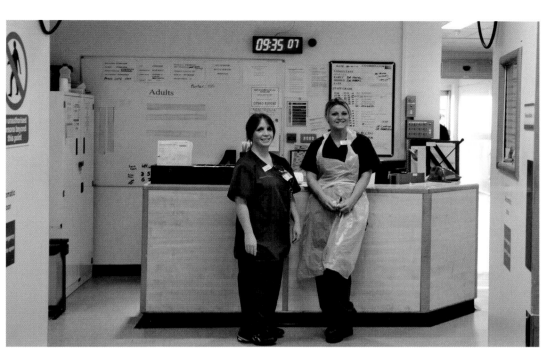

White Coats
(*Above*) Nurses in the Emergency Department of Colchester General Hospital, anxiously waiting for an ambulance, manage half smiles for the camera. (*Below*) The CT scanner at Colchester General Hospital whose operators are not visible to the camera. *Photographs*: Martin Gould.

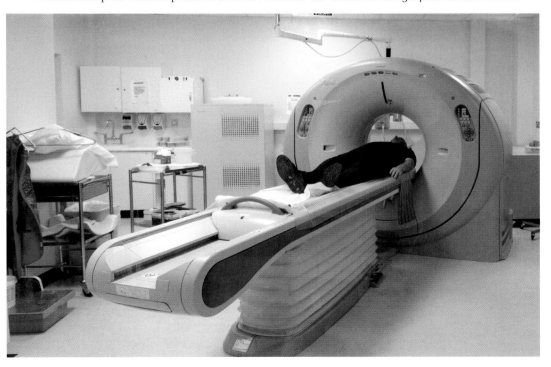

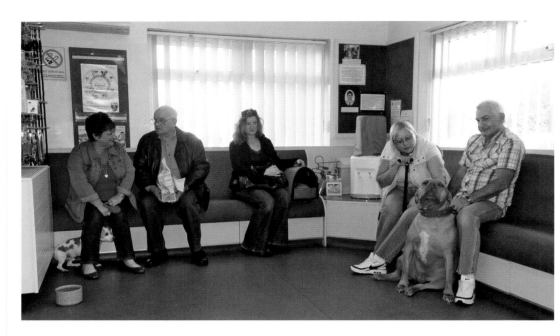

Veterinary

(*Above*) Owners and pets wait with customary British patience for their turn to be seen by the vet in the Ark Veterinary Centre. Tammy the terrier (*left*) keeps a careful watch on Preston, the bullmastiff, (*far right*) as his owners Cheryl and Peter impart reassurance. (*Below*) Vet Jackie Pearson examines Poppy the Border terrier at the Colne Valley Veterinary Surgery. *Photographs*: Vic Hainsworth, Andrew Pearson.

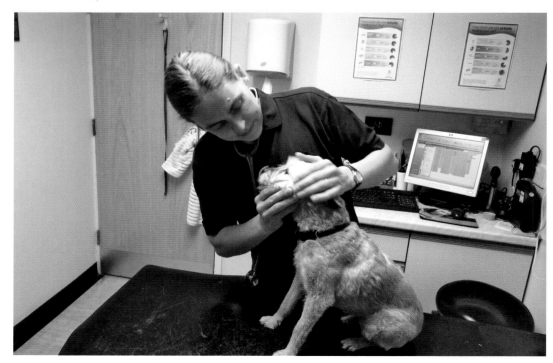

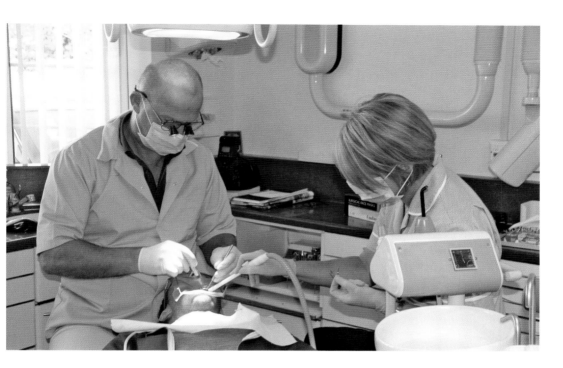

Needlework

Colchester has over thirty dental practices. At the Chesterfields Dental Partnership (*above*) Clive Bentley treats a patient, with assistance from Sharon. (*Below*) One in five British people have tattoos. Here, Colchester's long-serving tattooist Dave Ross in his picturesque, timbered Magdalen Street parlour completes a customer's first tattoo, a rose. *Photographs*: Vic Hainsworth, Andrew Phillips.

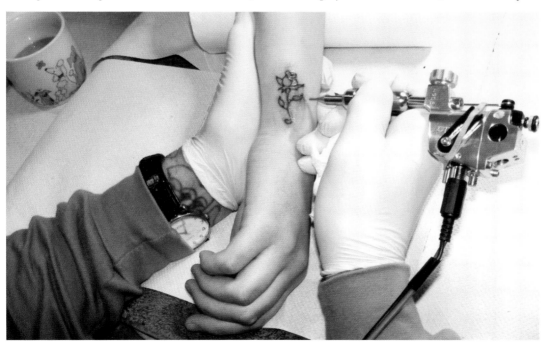

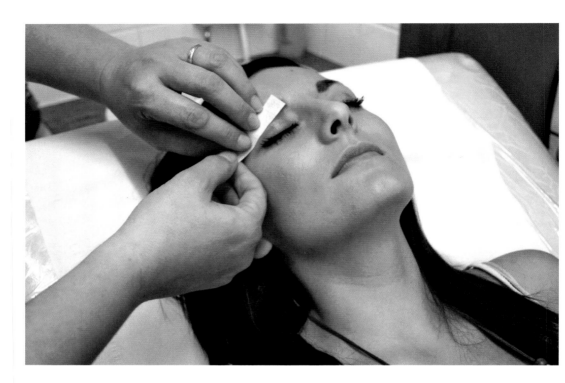

Pampering
Recent research shows there are now regional patterns to eyebrow shape in the UK. (*Above*) Jess has her eyebrows plucked at Hair and Body Additions at The Willows Shopping Centre. (Below) Daniel, a regular customer, lies in the sunbed at the Soleil Tanning & Beauty Salon. *Photographs*: Sioux Jordan.

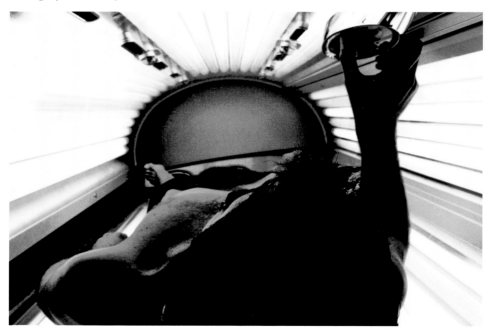

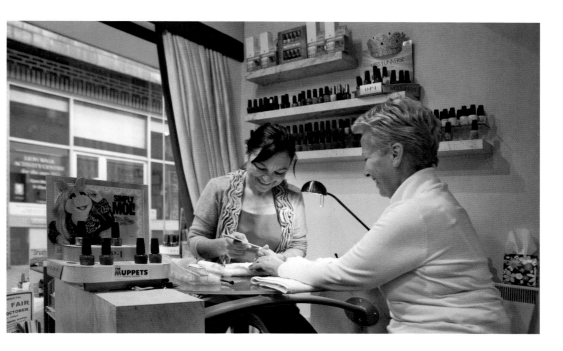

Grooming

(*Above*) At Simply Nails regular customers have their finger nails capped with fashion nails. These are then tinted. Note the selection of over 200 varnishes available to customers. (*Below*) This traditional barber's shop at St Botolph's Corner is busy on a Saturday morning. *Photographs*: Roy Essery, Andrew Phillips.

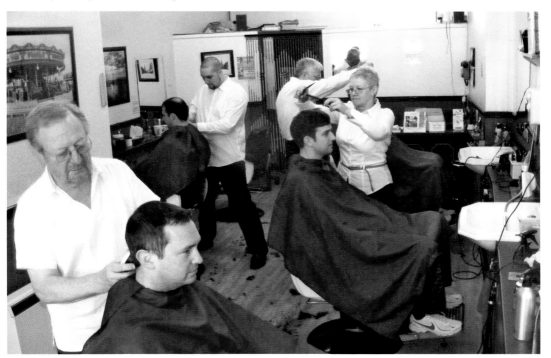

SHOPPING

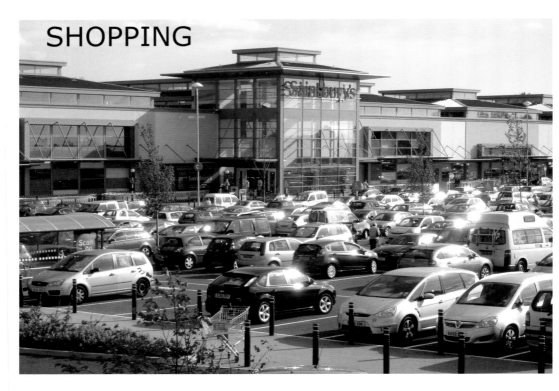

Shopping

Shopping is now deemed to be a national pastime, fulfilling many needs. Food shopping at a large supermarket usually requires a car, hence (*above*) the 800-space car park of Colchester's largest supermarket, Sainsbury's with, (*below*), the wide choices offered in the fresh fruit and vegetables section. *Photographs*: Jill Raeburn Wilson.

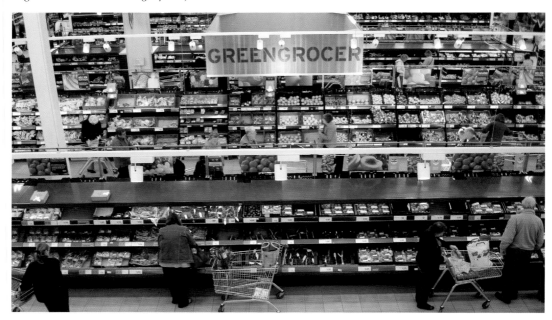

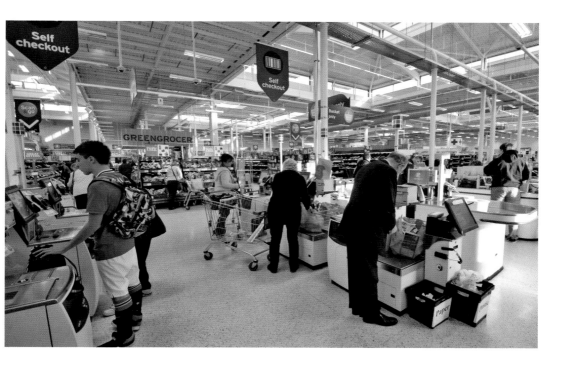

Paying

(*Above*) Self-service checkout is slowly becoming accepted. By scanning their own purchases, customers help cut costs for the stores. You can even scan as you go with a hand-held scanner. (*Below*) A Saturday morning queue at a cash machine in Culver Street East, a familiar sight in 2011, is stalled by three men with backpacks wrestling to cope with the challenge. *Photographs*: Mick Murton, Chris Farndell.

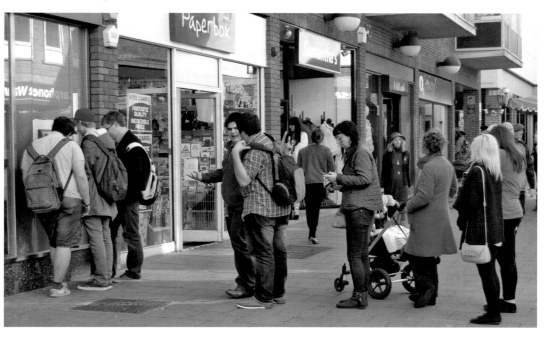

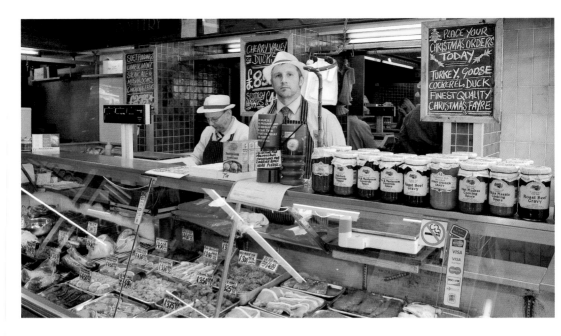

Specialising (1)

Colchester shops are mainly surviving the recession. (*Above*) Geller's has been a butcher's shop for sixty-seven years. Despite sauces on the counter and pasties made on the premises, there is little change in what they mainly sell: meat, displayed to the high standards of today. (*Below*) Mr Simms Olde Sweet Shoppe seeks to recall a world we have lost and offers a range of nostalgic treats in rows of plastic jars. *Photographs*: Dave Clarke, John Soliven.

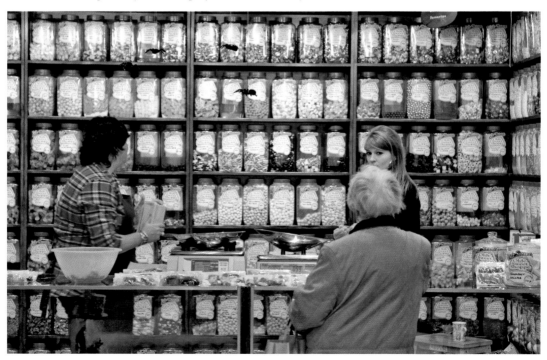

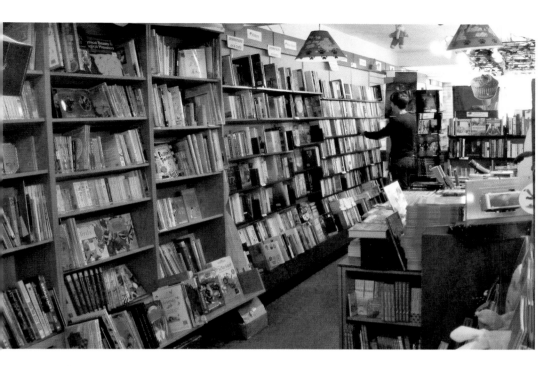

Specialising (2)

Building a business is a massive investment in time and effort. (*Above*) Red Lion Bookshop, founded in 1978, has twice been voted Independent Bookshop of the Year. Its website reveals a host of promotions and special events to bolster its sale of books. (*Below*) Andrews TV, in business since 1980, sell and repair televisions, and specialise in audio equipment. Their shop, full of widescreen LCD TVs, is characteristic of our time. *Photographs*: Andrew Phillips.

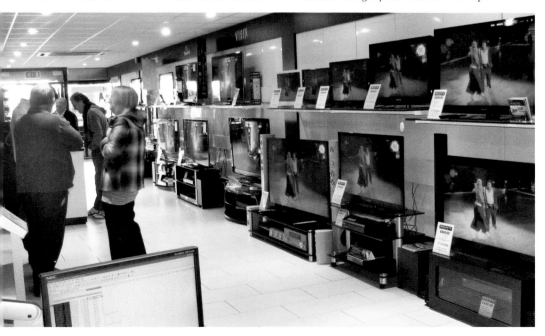

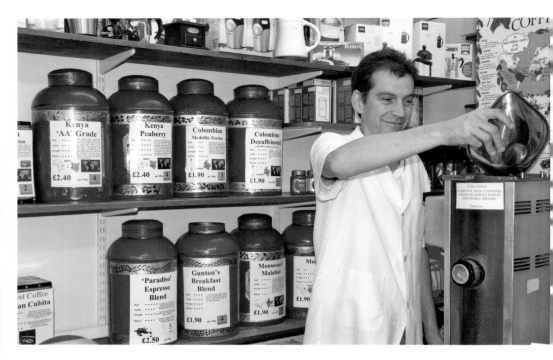

Specialising (3)

(*Above*) Phil Gunton, whose great-grandfather founded the well-known Crouch Street delicatessen in 1936, grinds coffee from the firm's extensive range of beans, all of which are roasted on the premises. (*Below*) Michael sorts a few of the 400 bikes on sale at Cycle King of East Gate. *Photographs*: Mark Whiting, Andrew Phillips.

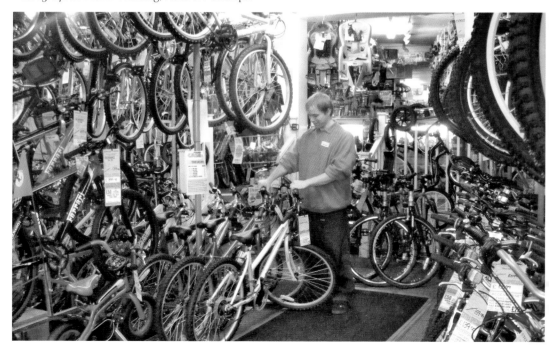

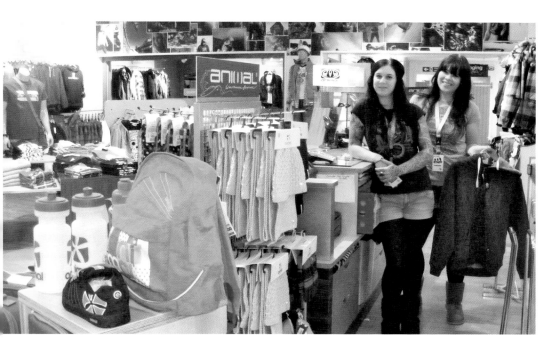

Clothing

(*Above*) Animal, a brand of casual sportswear mainly for the young, has fifty stores nationwide. Sarah and Catherine staff the Colchester shop. (*Below*) Michael and Shaun stand by the men's suits offered by Moss in High Street. Previously known as Moss Bros, the firm has traded since 1898 and was founded by a descendant of Eliazor Moses, who pioneered the mass-production of men's clothes, one of Colchester's contributions to the Industrial Revolution. *Photographs:* Andrew Phillips.

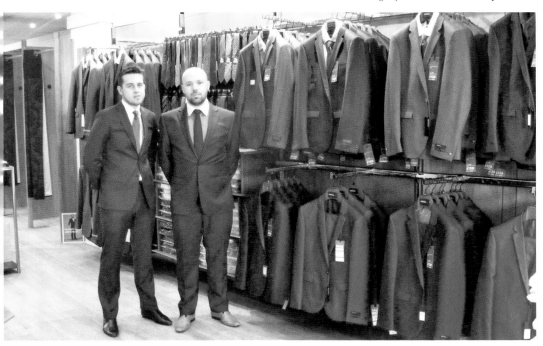

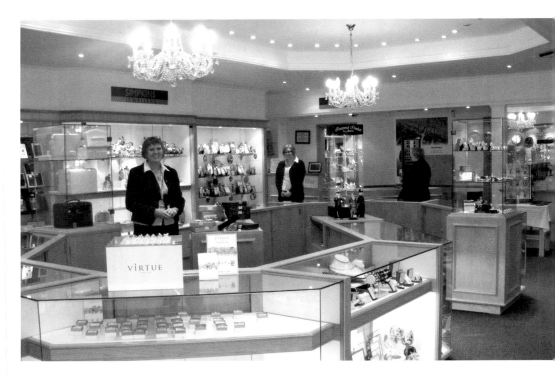

Investing

The bright, protected interior of traditional jeweller's, Simpkins (*above*), once found in all shops, survives here as a discouragement to theft. (*Below*) No, not a hotel reception, but a modern betting shop, Ladbrokes. Computers, the Internet and new legislation have facilitated major growth in the gambling industry. *Photographs*: Andrew Phillips, Richard Lyon.

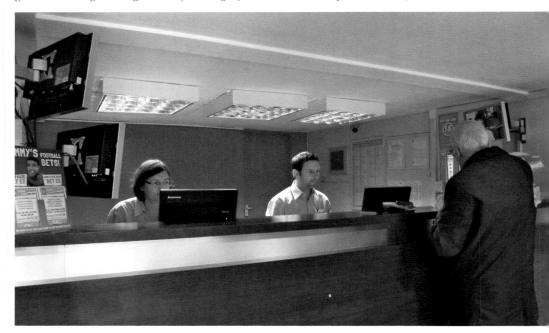

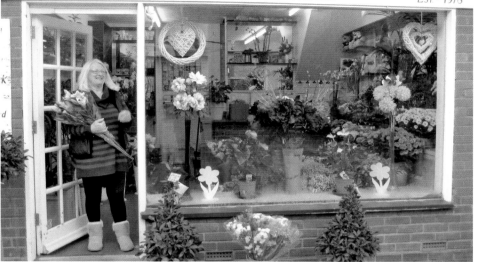

Indulging

Colchester has a wealth of small shops. Here are just two, highlighting the range of goods on offer. (*Above*) Carol stands in the doorway of the florist she has worked in for twenty years. 'It's a good job', she says, 'you make people happy.' (*Below*) Roly's fudge is made on the premises. The shop supplies all the fudge for Southend Pier and for Ipswich FC. *Photographs*: Philip Crummy.

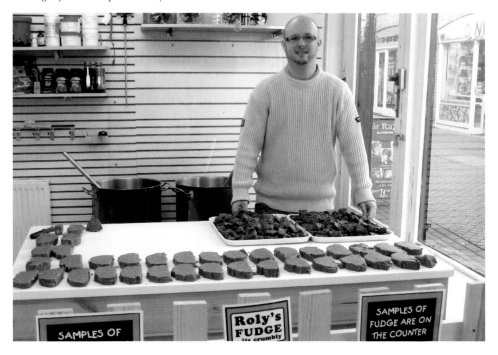

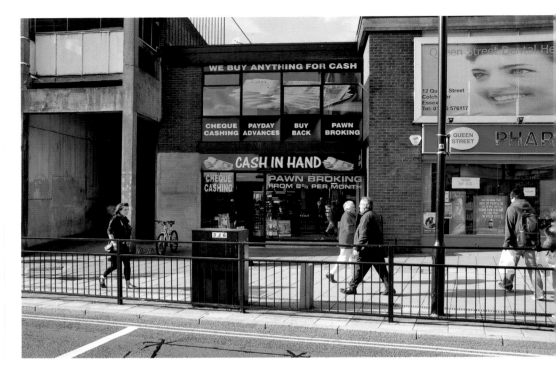

Economising

The recession of the last few years has seen a growth in two types of shops. (*Above*) A new-style pawn broker. (*Below*) A special version of the 'Pound Shop' – where everything costs £1 – which flourishes every Christmas, installed in a former sports shop. On 22 October 2011 this one stands open. *Photographs*: Dave Clarke, Frankie Olano.

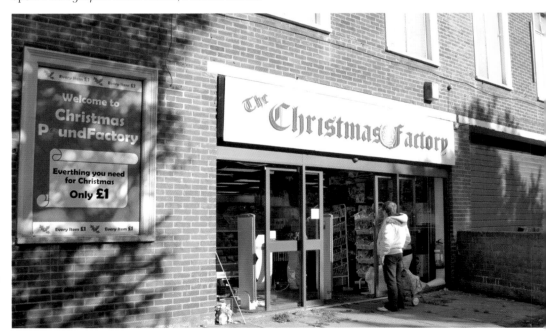

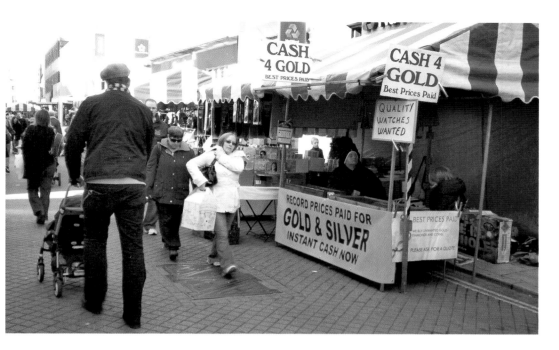

Markets (1)
Every weekend market stalls spread down Culver Street and round Trinity Square. (*Above*) The Recession, the high price of gold and the need for ready cash, keeps this stall going. The owner sees it as an extension of his hobby – collecting and trading in coins. (*Below*) Pavement sales include magazines, spectacles, mobile phone covers and this enterprising footwear display. *Photographs*: Kath Tobin, Dave Clarke.

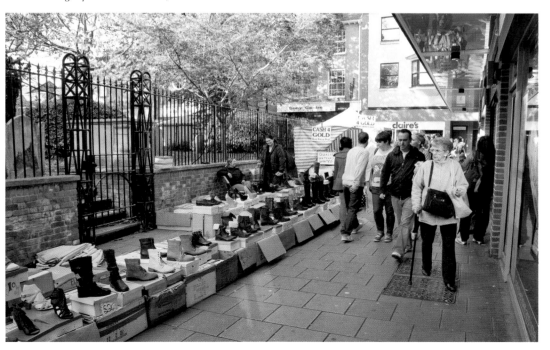

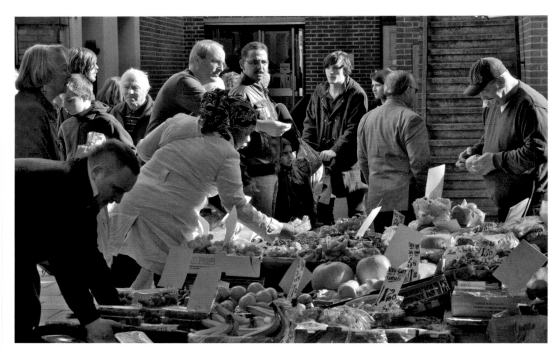

Markets (2)

(*Above*) This Saturday fruit and vegetable stall is doing a flourishing trade. Customers' faces reflect the serious business of selecting the best offers. (*Below*) Customers study the best points of a chicken at the Severalls Lane Market. *Photographs*: Phil Brew, Andrew Pearson.

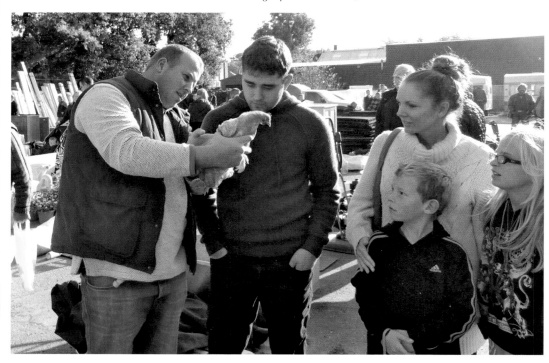

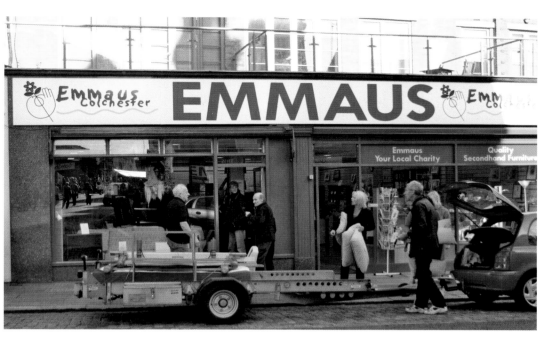

Charity

The rise of charity shops in Colchester has been marked since 1986. (*Above*) Emmaus, a charity which helps the homeless, opened this High Street shop in 2009. As this photograph shows, unwanted furniture is especially welcome. (*Below*) Tony and Bruce prepare for a jumble sale in St Martin's Church in the Dutch Quarter to raise money for the victims of the famine in Somalia. *Photographs*: Simona Szakacs, Phil Brew.

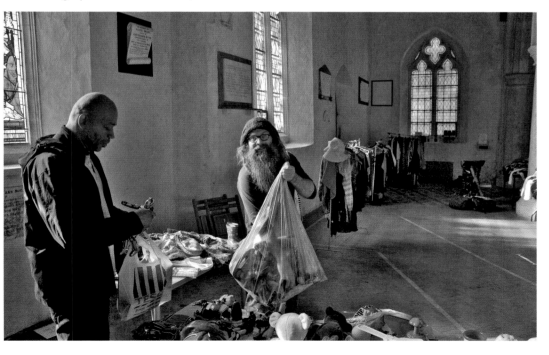

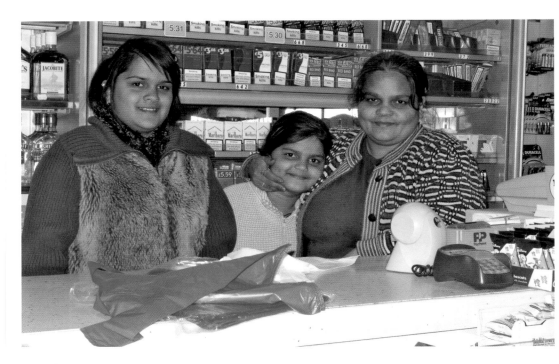

Out of Town

(*Above*) Corner stores and convenience shops still abound. Many are run by Asian families, who put in long hours to sustain their businesses. (*Above*) Mrs Patel and her husband have run this store for years, but the next generation, their two daughters, have other ambitions. (*Below*) Home delivery of food is an expanding business. This Tesco van supplies 'next day' delivery, a considerable boon to the elderly. *Photographs*: Amit Roy, Kath Tobin.

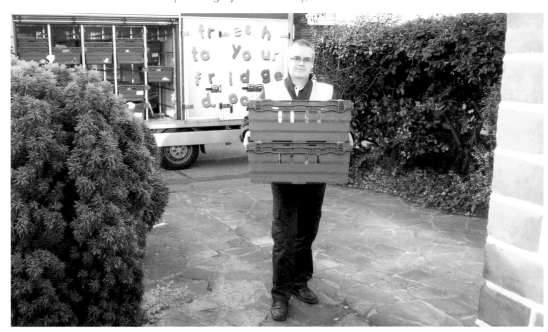

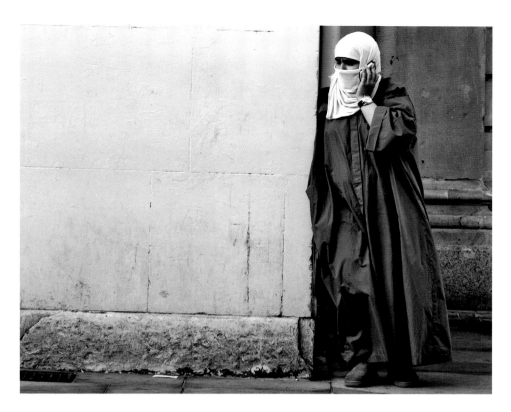

Multiculturalism

Colchester's streets in 2011 also record another important change: Colchester is becoming ethnically diverse. A university, language schools, ethnic restaurants and migrant workers add to the total, as do permanent residents. (*Above*) A traditional black robe and a hijab go with a mobile phone and modern watch. (*Below*) Three faces in North Station Road. *Photographs*: John Soliven, Phil Brew.

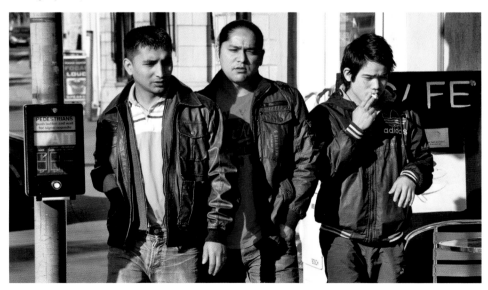

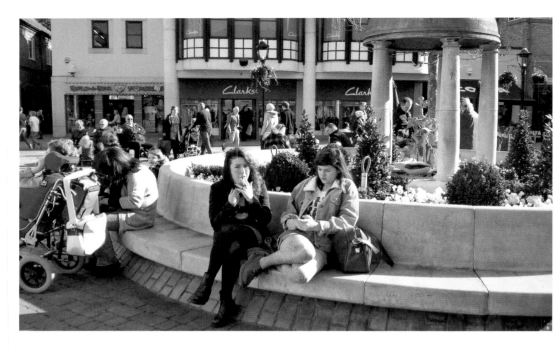

Relaxing

'Going to town' is not solely about shopping. It is also an experience; the chance to have lunch or a beer, to be seen or to see. (*Above*) Culver Square provides a regular place for relaxation; to smoke or to check your smartphone. (*Below*) Sitting over a cup of coffee, watching the world go by, is another universal activity made possible by more outdoor seating. *Photographs*: Kath Tobin, Chris Farndell.

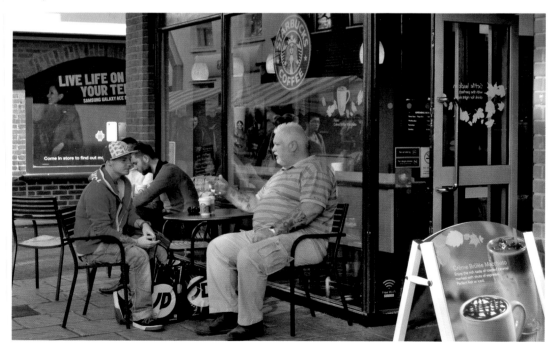

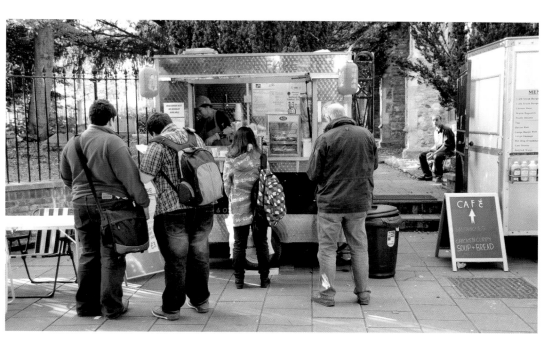

Snacking

Since 1986 small food kiosks have successfully established themselves in Colchester at weekends along Culver Street and in Trinity Square. This stall (*above*) run by Wei sells Chinese food. The most popular dish, she says, is noodles. (*Below*) Out at Gosbeck's Road, Mick (*left*) and Stewart (*right*) enjoy the custom supplied by Mark Hartley's Angry Onion burger van. *Photographs*: Dave Clarke, Ivan Beales.

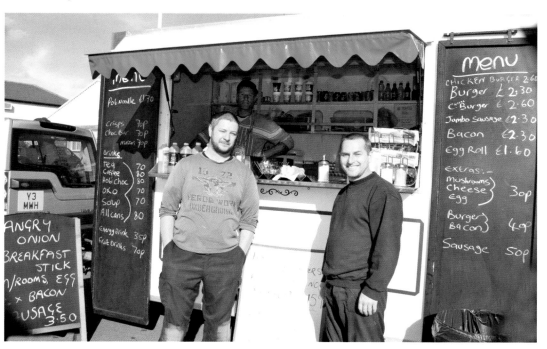

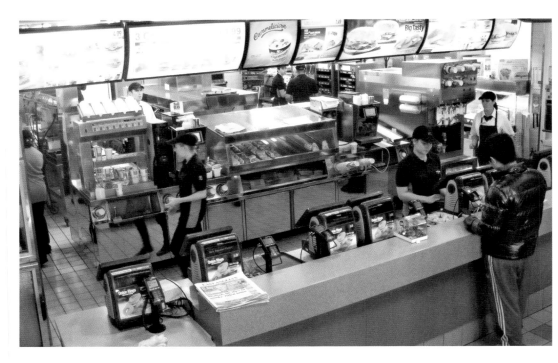

Eating Out

(*Above*) Streamlined food preparation at the McDonald's in High Street. Shiny overhead panels carry alluring views of possible dishes, and staff move efficiently through their divisions of labour. (*Below*) A waitress eye view of the Cameo Café, selling everything from fruit to a full English. *Photographs*: Andrew Phillips, Alan Murrells.

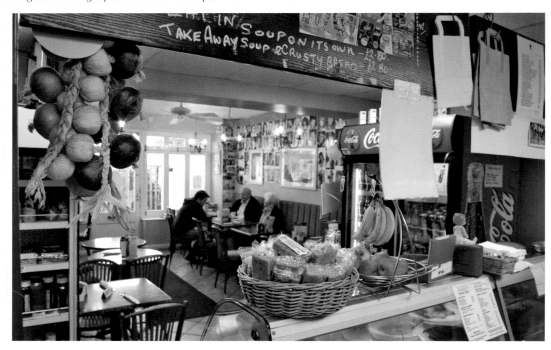

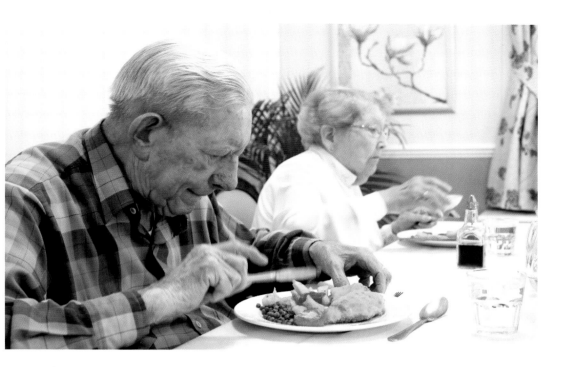

Eating In

Public care for the elderly is a growing Colchester need, made more pressing in 2011 by funding restraints on Essex County Council. The Balkerne Garden Trust is a well known independent provision, with its forty-bedded residential facility in Freda Gunton Lodge and sixty-nine sheltered housing flats. (*Above*) Former mayor and mayoress of Colchester, Westley and Lila Sandford, enjoy a fish and chip lunch. (*Below*) A general view of the dining area. *Photographs:* Fran Dale, Jenny Rudd.

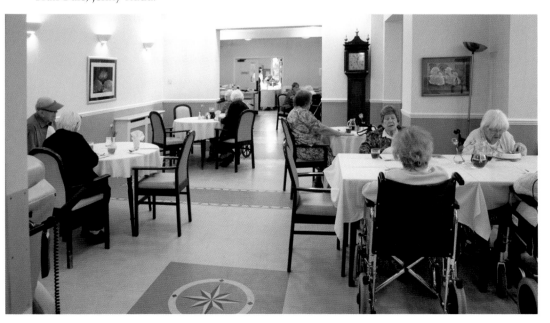

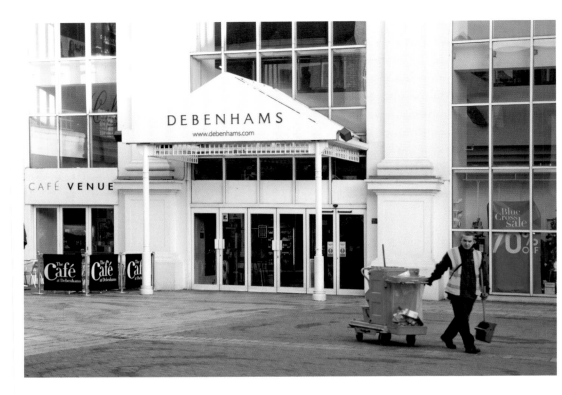

Closing Time

(*Above*) As shops close for the day the Culver Precinct is swept by its own staff. Behind sits Colchester's landmark department store, Debenhams. (*Below*) Going home can involve a bus queue. Behind this one in Queen Street sits a dramatic piece of commissioned wall art, completed in 2011. Unfortunately the bus stop, timetable and shelter in front of it, renders the street art less than accessible. *Photographs*: Roy Essery, Paul Douglas.

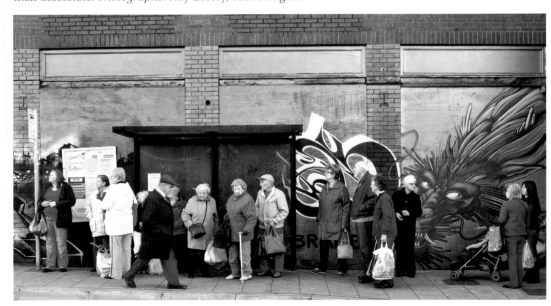

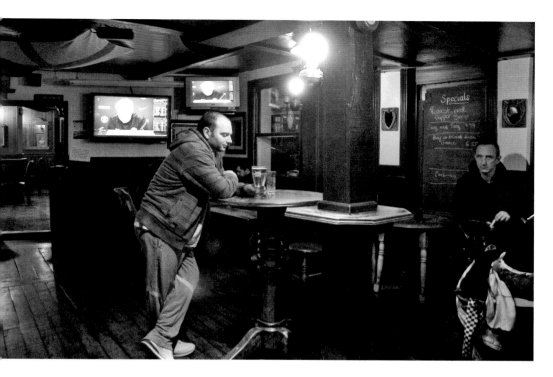

Pubs: Contemplation

Since 1986 a number of Colchester pubs have closed; others have suffered bewildering name changes, yet fifty-one remain. (*Above*) Beneath the mindless television screens, a lone drinker nurses his beer. (*Below*) Beside the pool table of the TP Sports Bar, two men, interrupted by the photographer, pause in their conversation. *Photographs*: Richard Lyon, Andy Brooke.

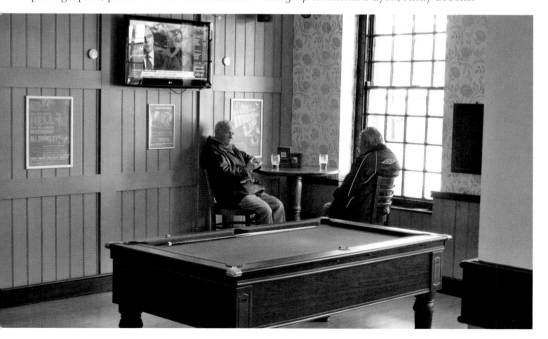

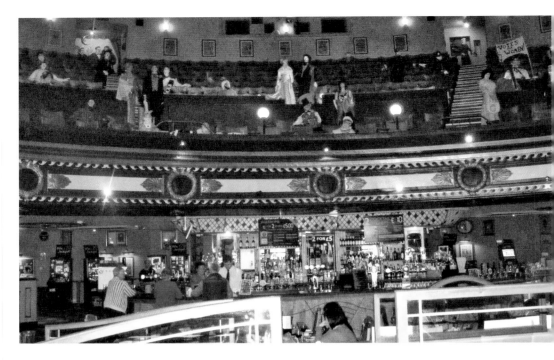

Pubs: Animation

(*Above*) Colchester's largest pub, the Playhouse, opened as a theatre in 1929, became a cinema, and then a bingo hall. In 1994 it opened as a pub, but the architects retained the theatre's gallery. From the main eating area one can look up at a band of ghostly, spot-lit Edwardians in the gallery seats. (*Below*) Another busy pub, the Castle Inn. Four quiet drinkers right, three left, and centre an animated cluster of the young. Evening has come. *Photographs*: Andrew Phillips, Richard Lyon.

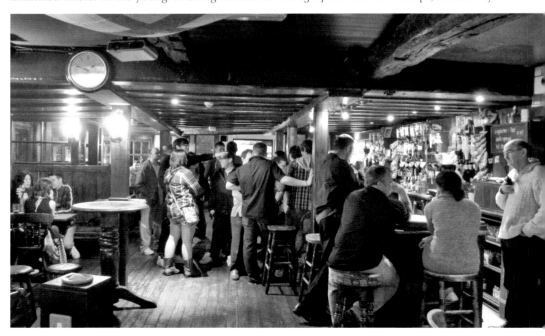

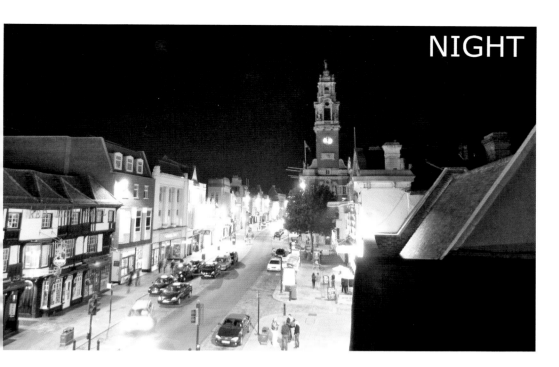

NIGHT

Night

Midnight on the Town Hall clock – the halfway point of *Colchester 24*. The High Street is virtually deserted, apart from taxis, which gather in numbers at the rank. (*Below*) Two military police guard the town. When the Colchester Garrison was established in 1857, the sometimes riotous behaviour of soldiers made military police a nightly necessity. Today they supply a presence, and patrol the night. *Photographs*: Richard Lyon and Sgt Rupert Frere.

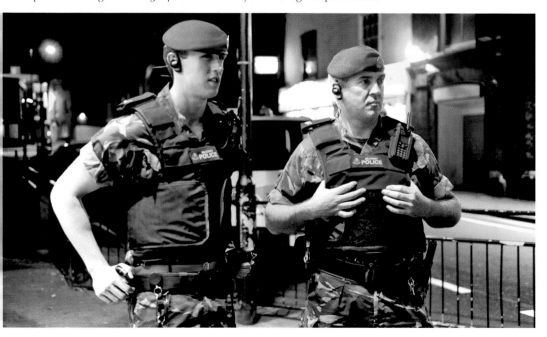

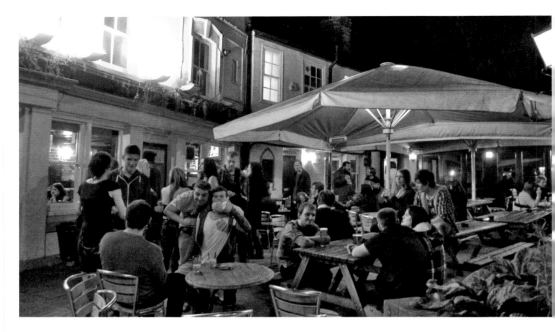

Pubs & Clubs

With its large outdoor seating area and closeness to High Street, the Castle pub (*above*) is always heaving with drinkers. At the other end of High Street stands the imposing Yates's bar (*below*), one of Colchester's most popular nightspots. The bar doubles up as a club in the evenings, when live DJs take to the stage and the tables and chairs make way for a dance floor. *Photographs*: Richard Lyon.

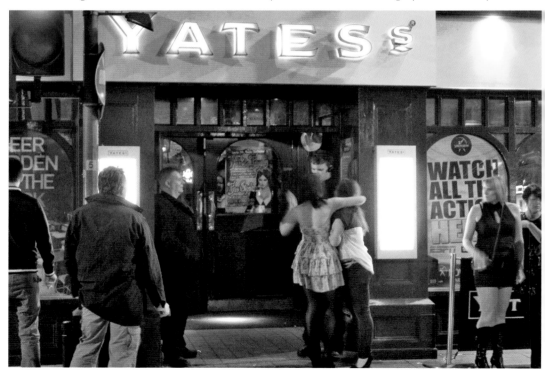

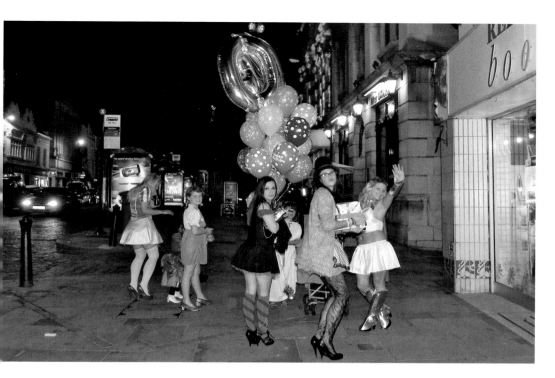

Revellers

Above, a group of ladies totter along the High Street in their high heels, wearing fancy dress, on their way to a 40th birthday party celebration. Up the other end of the High Street three musicians (*below*) entice passers-by to have a dance before moving on. *Photographs*: Richard Lyon.

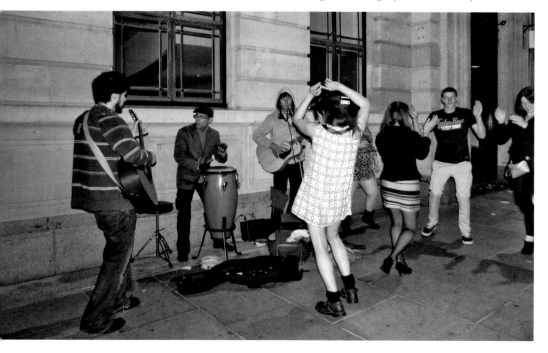

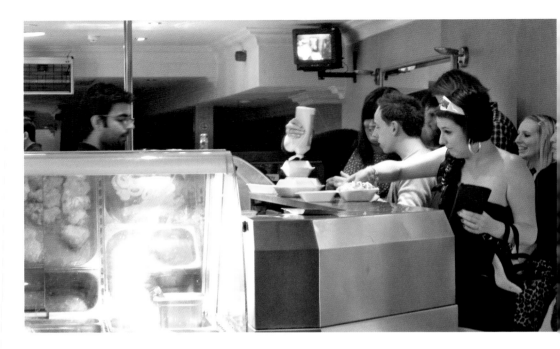

Peckish at 2am?
Colchester's town centre caters to all tastes, with a host of take-away joints and places to grab a quick bite. (*Above*) Clubbers stop in at Big Man's Fish & Grill on the High Street at 2.37 a.m. to enjoy a nutritious serving of cheesy chips. The Continental Supermarket (*below*) sells everything from cigarettes to baked beans. Specialising in Eastern European produce, the supermarket adds to the town's embraced multiculturalism. *Photographs*: Richard Lyon, Paul Douglas.

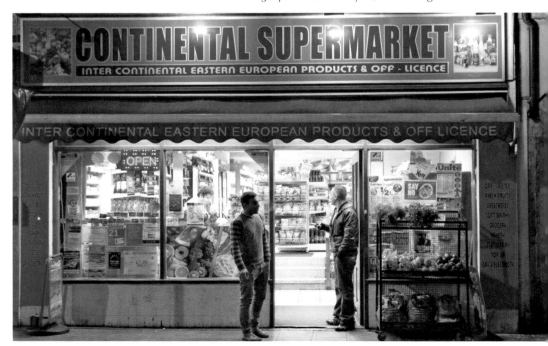

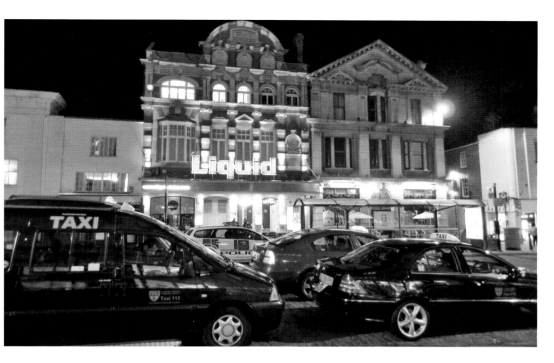

Taxi?

Colchester's biggest and brashest club, Liquid, dominates the late-night High Street with its neon signage and constant police presence. Newly refurbished, the club always attracts hundreds of people raring to make use of the large dance floor and the cheap champagne. (*Below*) At the end of a night on the town, the taxi rank on High Street becomes the busiest place in Colchester, as people desperately try to make their way home. *Photographs*: Richard Lyon.

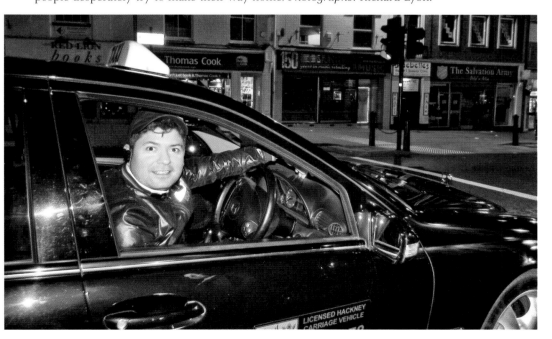

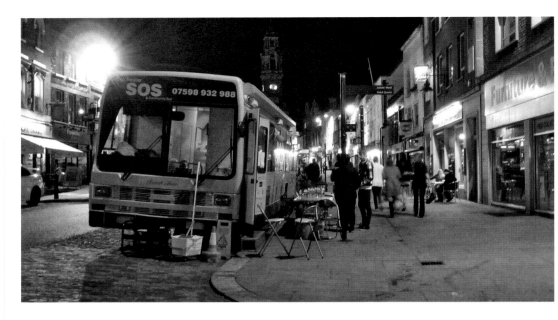

SOS

(*Above*) Launched in 2008, the SOS Bus serves Colchester's late-night population. Every Friday and Saturday night, the St John's Ambulance volunteers hand out water and make sure people have a safe place to sit and recover. (*Below*) Colchester has a significant number of homeless people. It is now a familiar sight, both day and night, to see people sleeping rough in doorways around the town centre. *Photographs*: Maria Goodman, Richard Lyon.

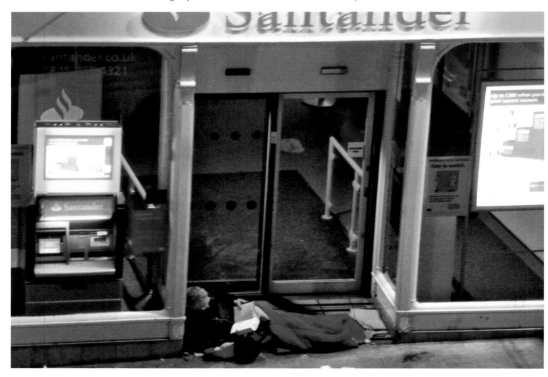

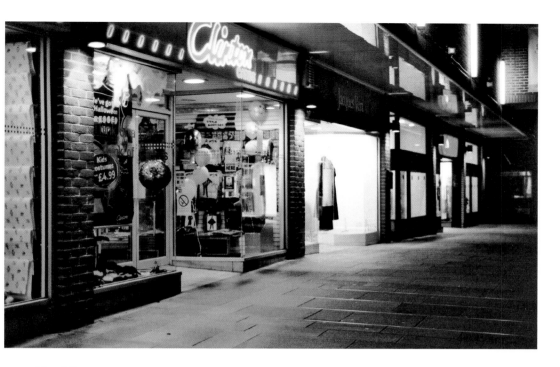

Ghost Town

The inner streets of Colchester shut down for the evening as people bypass the closed shops and stick to the fringes, where bars and restaurants abound. The shop lights stay on and keep the Lion Walk Precinct (*above*) illuminated throughout the night. However Eld Lane and Short Wyre Street's older shop fronts and buildings (*below*) stay masked in darkness. The light at the end of the tunnel is St Botolph's Street, which is full of eateries and bars. *Photographs*: Remy Gopaul, Richard Lyon.

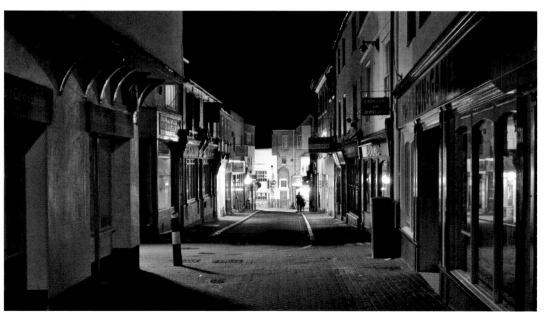

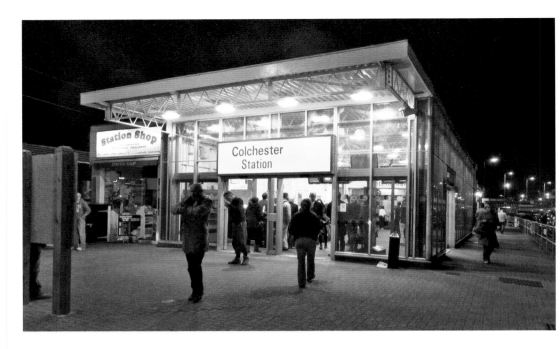

Travellers in the Night (1)

Commuters stream home from a busy day in London. North Station (*above*), on the main line to London, is Colchester's busiest train station. Supermarkets, including Tesco (*below*), offer a 24-hour petrol service to fuel their customers' needs, day or night. You can now pay at the pump, a system which has helped petrol stations cut back on their need for staff. *Photographs*: Andrew Pearson, Paul Douglas.

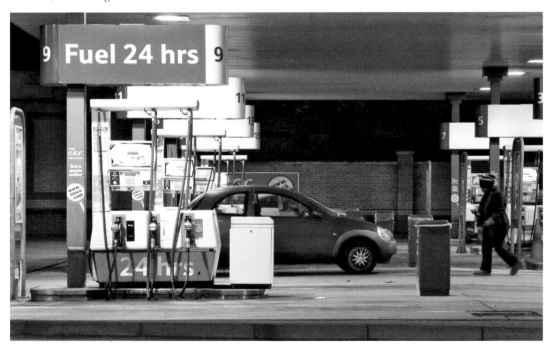

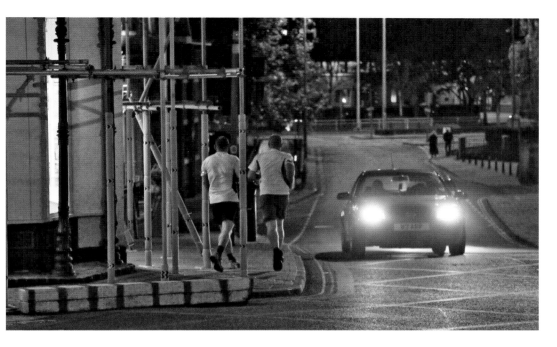

Travellers in the Night (2)

(*Above*) Two night joggers run past Headgate Corner on their way through the town. Only a short way out of its centre, Colchester has a wealth of public walkways that offer runners and cyclists safe, brightly lit and well maintained paths on which to walk and cycle. The walkway (*below*) links the town to the University of Essex, whose towers shine brightly in the night, two miles from the town centre. *Photographs*: Paul Douglas and Mark Cave.

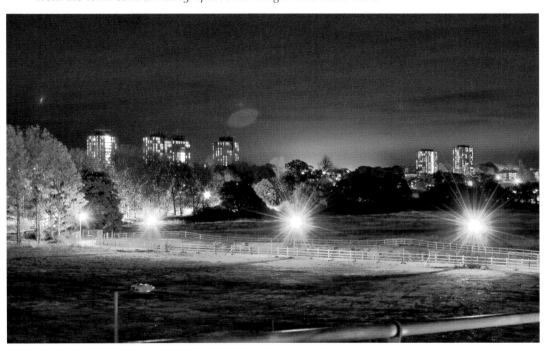

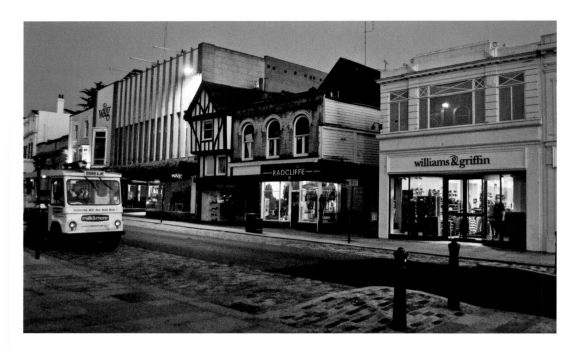

Dawn

(*Above*) 6 a.m. a milkman delivers. Radcliffe's, the High Street's oldest business, established as a gun shop in 1812, sits sandwiched between two arms of Williams & Griffin, a home-grown department store. Plans are afoot to relocate Radcliffe's into a rebuilt W & G, offering 'London shopping'. (*Below*) 7 a.m. a man lies prone on a bench before a glamorous window display. The day has begun. *Photographs*: Steven Harper, Roy Essery.

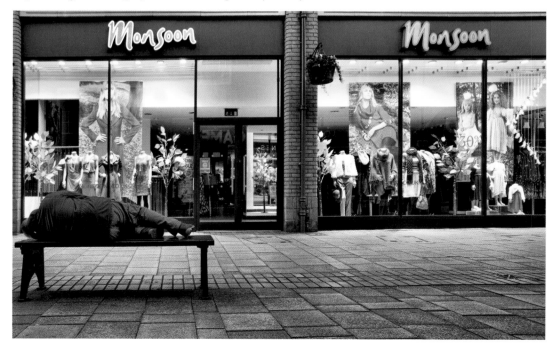

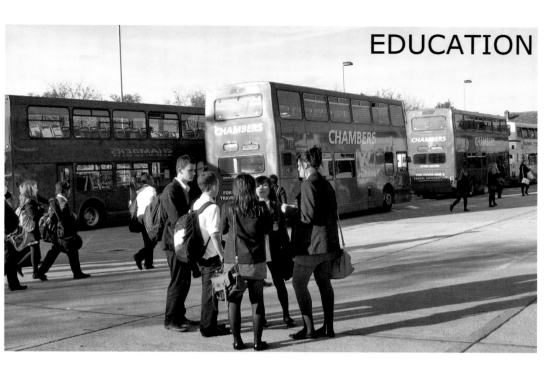

Education

(*Above*) Dozens of buses pick up hundreds of students from St Benedict's College and the Colchester County High School for Girls every afternoon. Norman Way becomes a frenzied mass of vehicles, all trying to escape the traffic jam that builds up along Lexden Road. (*Below*) Education begins at birth; reading ideally begins at home. Jan, a registered childminder, reads to sisters Ruby (aged three) and Chloe (aged eight months). *Photographs*: Joan Rew, Chris Simmonds.

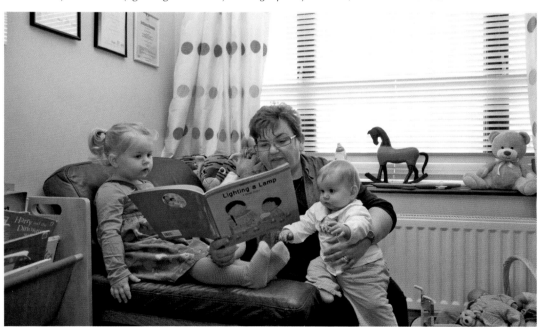

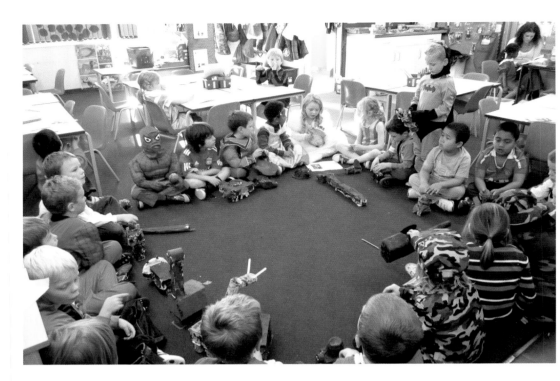

Reception

(*Above*) The reception class at St John's Primary School sits dressed as their favourite book characters, explaining to their class mates why they have chosen them. (*Below*) Phoebe helps Katie in 'buddy reading,' where children listen to each other read and help each other understand any difficult parts. *Photographs*: Nick Hutchings.

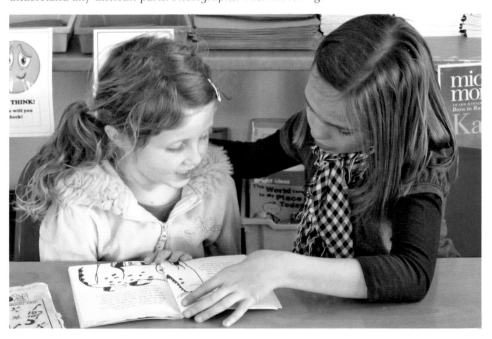

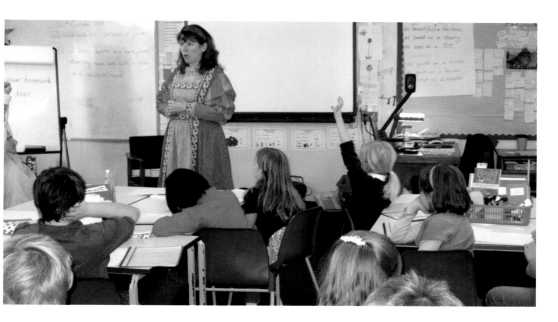

Fancy Dress

(*Above*) Dressed as a Tudor queen, Ms Berrie teaches Year 4 children about the Tudors. (*Below*) Being picked up by Mum is a common infant school experience: three pupils of Oxford House, the Lexden Road private school, in their distinctive uniforms. *Photographs*: Nick Hutchings, Andrew Phillips.

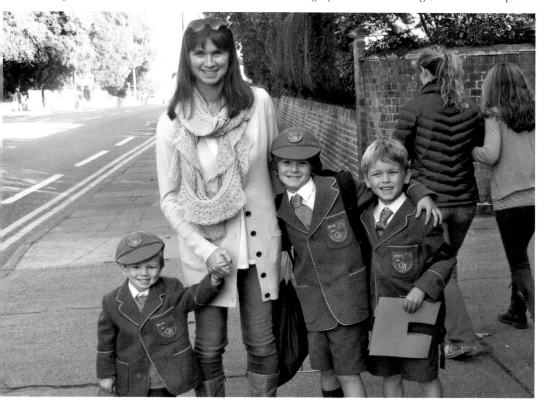

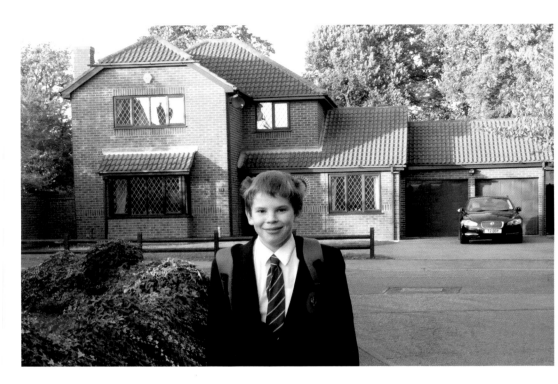

Adolescence

My home, my school: Year 7 student Samuel (*above*) proudly shows off his Gilberd School uniform as he stands in front of his house. (*Below*) A group of youngsters from the Thomas Lord Audley School discuss the day's events sitting on the pavement in the Willows shopping area in Monkwick. *Photographs*: Andrew Pearson, Sioux Jordan.

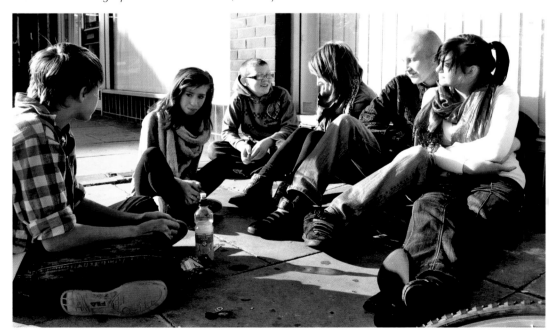

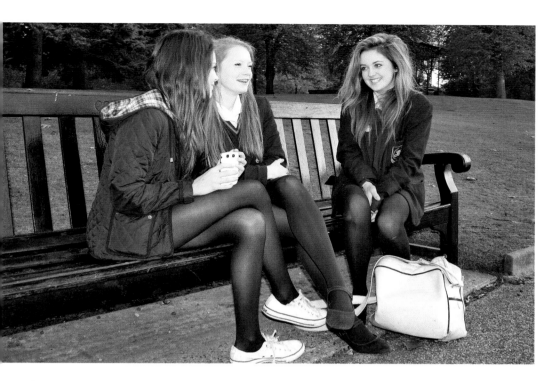

Teenagers

Characteristic traits of teenagers: the girls sit close together, deep in conversation, clearly a little wary of the photographer who has disrupted them, whereas the boys engage the photographer in a brazen show of camaraderie. The girls are poised and self-conscious; the boys are full of confidence and swagger. *Photographs*: Nikki Hazelton, Alan Murrells.

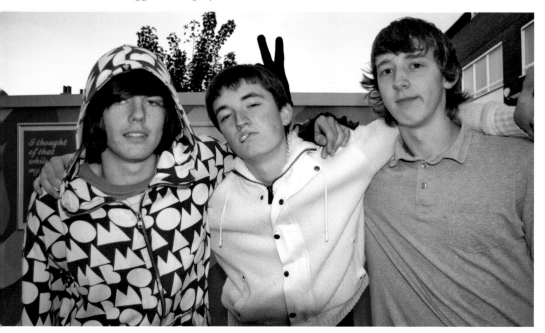

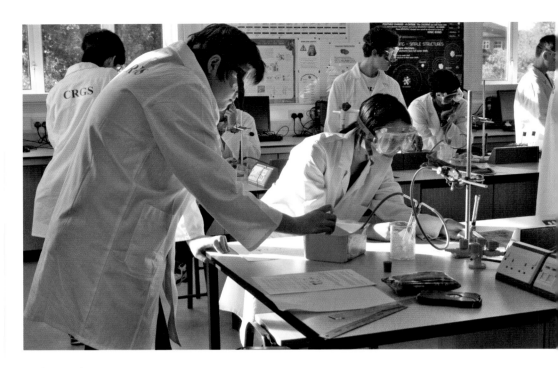

In the Sixth Form

(*Above*) Anna and William take part in an AS level Chemistry class at Colchester Royal Grammar School. Since 1998 girls have been allowed to enter the school's previously boys-only sixth form. (*Below*) An A level Art class at Colchester Sixth Form College, where students are doing individual work for their coursework. The Visual Arts Department has about 800 students each year. *Photographs*: Sue Barber and Andy Brooke.

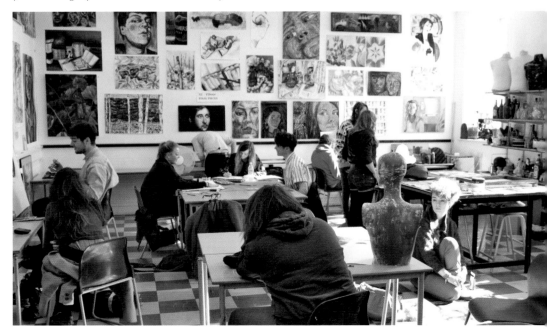

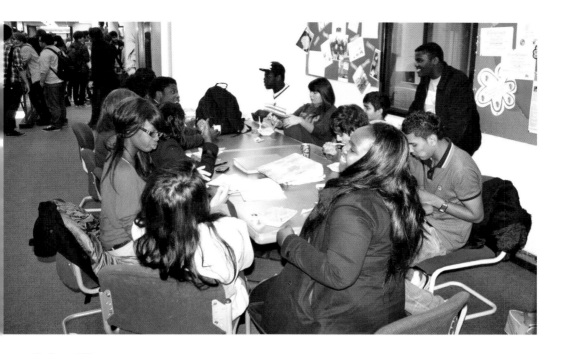

College Life

Founded in 1987 and recruiting from a wide area, Colchester Sixth Form College is a considerable success story, with nearly 1,000 students gaining places in Higher Education each year. Its new buildings provide both for specialist education needs and for student socialising. A group of students (*above*) sit together in the College Concourse, grabbing lunch and finalising last-minute work. (*Below*) At the end of the college day students pour out onto North Hill. *Photographs*: Andy Brooke, Adrian Rushton.

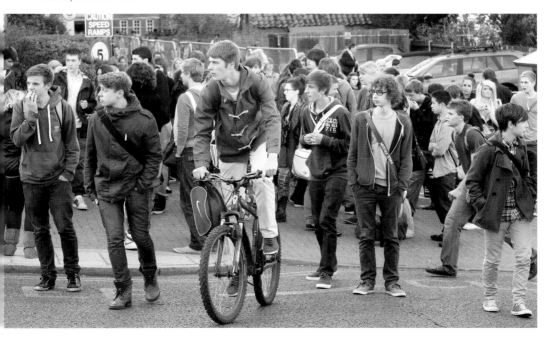

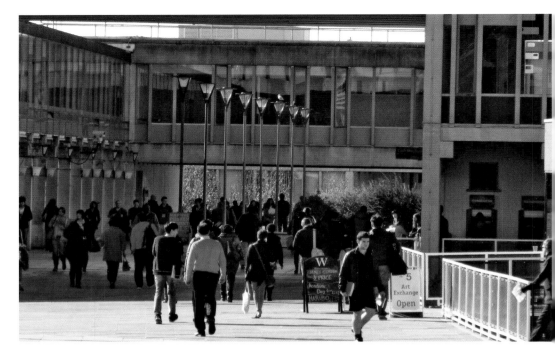

Campus Life

Built in the 1960s, the University of Essex's characteristic concrete-and-glass architecture has stood the test of time. (*Above*) Students go from one square to another in the hub of the University. A bookshop, cash machines, restaurants and art galleries are all clustered here. (*Below*) From left to right, Aurelia, Sarah and Farrah enjoy a night out in Sub Zero, the University's award-winning nightclub. *Photographs*: Amalia Mihailescu, Farrah Mombongo.

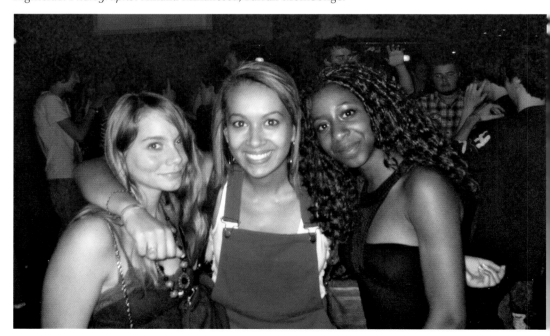

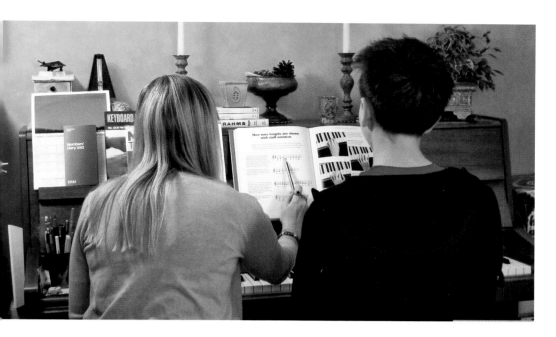

Further Education

(*Above*) Celia Parker-Wilson teaches her son Wesley to read music in the music room of their home in Shrub End. Learning to play the piano has been a long-established middle-class tradition. (*Below*) 'Silver Surfers' research family history online at the Wilson Marriage Centre. Living longer has helped expand education for the retired age group. *Photographs*: Jill Raeburn-Wilson, David Robinson.

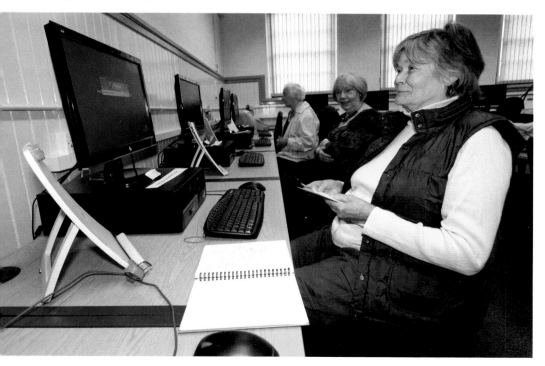

LEISURE

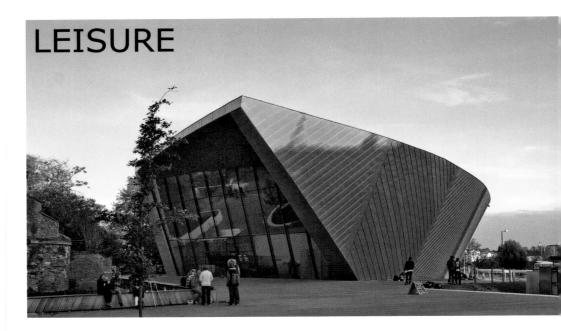

Firstsite

Firstsite, Colchester's new contemporary art gallery, opened in 2011 to much fanfare. Housed in a spectacular building designed by renowned architect Rafael Viñoly, its golden exterior is its most striking feature. However, its considerable expense and revolutionary design both generated criticism, as did the threat to the town's bus station that accompanied it. *Colchester 24* photographers captured its pristine splendour in a host of images, from which we have chosen three. *Photographs*: Lynda Robinson, Laurence Tobin.

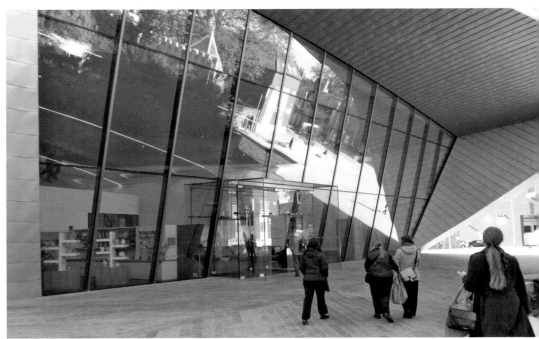

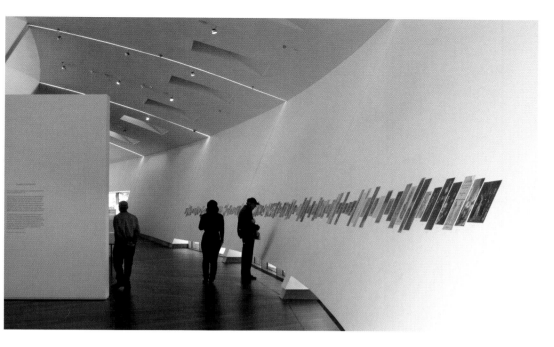

Sight & Sound

(*Above*) Firstsite's inaugural exhibition contained works of art by such luminaries as Henry Moore and Grayson Perry. However, probably the most popular exhibit, entitled 'Hello Colchester', a long line of images of famous individuals related to Colchester history, carrying the story down to the present day. (*Below*) The *Breakfast* presenter Gary Mulligan peers into Studio 1 at Dream 100FM radio to see *Drivetime* presenter Jonathan Murphy. Broadcasting from St Peter's, Dream 100 serves the whole of North Essex. *Photographs*: Laurence Tobin, Joff Hopkins.

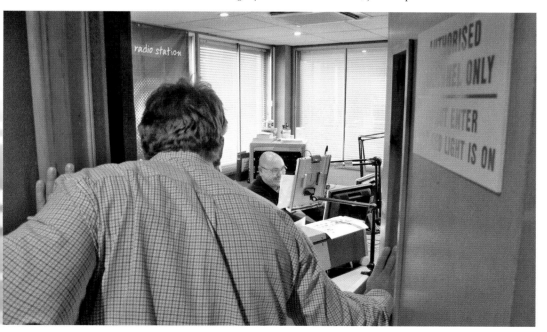

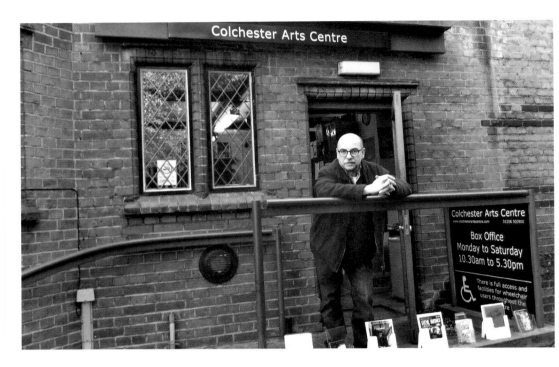

Live Shows

Colchester Arts Centre in the former St Mary at the Walls Church, is the town's premier live performance venue. Above stands Anthony Roberts, the Centre's Director since 1991. The venue prides itself on the eclectic range of shows it puts on: concerts, comedians, food & drink festivals, poetry recitals, and films. (*Below*) Arts Centre staff get the venue ready for yet another live show. *Photographs*: Anthony Roberts, Alan Murrells.

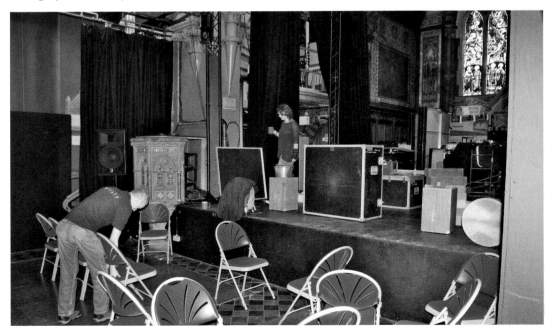

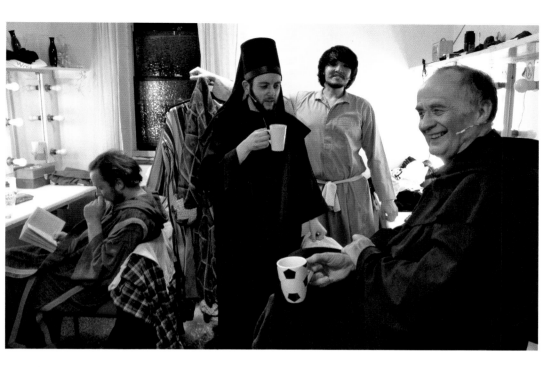

Song & Dance

(*Above*) The Colchester Operatic Society performs annually at the Mercury Theatre. Four cast members – Nathan, Rikki, Steve and John – take a breather during a performance of *Jesus Christ Superstar*. (*Below*) The Stage Coach Performing Arts Society holds their regular Saturday morning dance lesson at the sixth form college. The society offers private training for young aspiring actors and singers, aged four to eighteen. *Photographs*: Sam Pilkington, Andy Brooke.

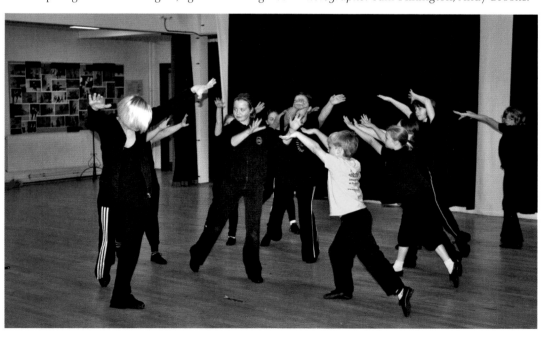

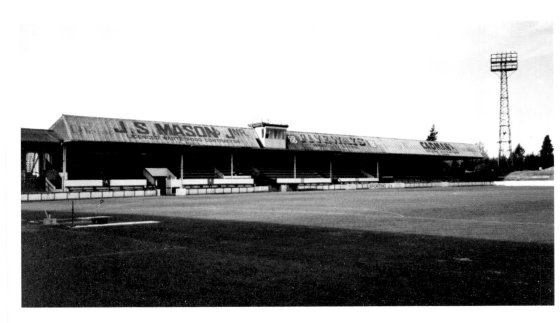

CUFC

Photographed in 1986 Layer Road (*above*) was Colchester United's home for seventy-one years. In 2008 the club finally upgraded to the Weston Homes Community Stadium (*below*), which has a capacity of 10,000 and much better training facilities, but is two miles from the town centre. Thoughtlessly, on 22 October 2011, the team had an away game, hence the empty seats. Meanwhile the Layer Road ground lies overgrown, awaiting the housing estate that is to be built there. *Photographs*: KC Eccles, Rebecca Sayer.

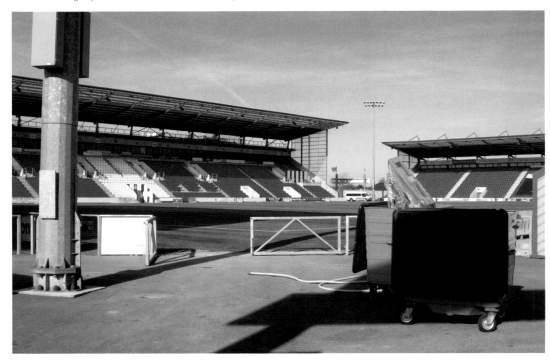

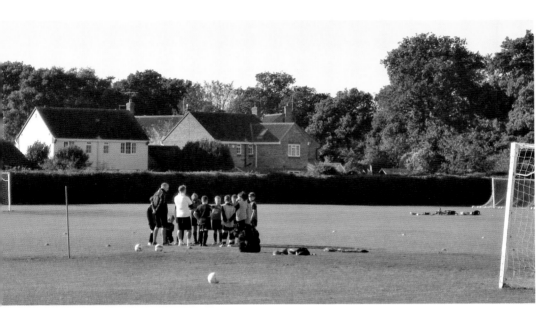

Team Sports

A typical scene on a Saturday morning is to see young people engaging in sports across the playing fields and sports clubs in and around Colchester. (*Above*) A football training session takes place on the fields at the end of Clairmont Road, Lexden. (*Below*) Young players engaged in a scrum at Colchester Rugby Club. Established in 1925, the Club boasts twenty teams, including colts', veterans' and ladies' teams. *Photographs*: Sarah Cole, Rebecca Sayer.

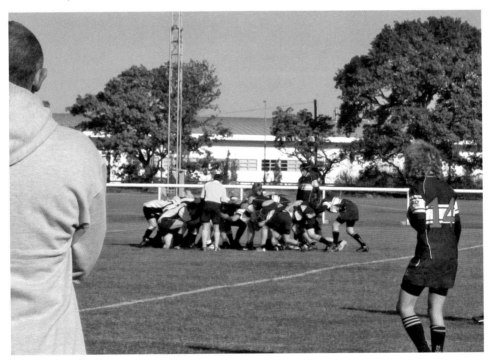

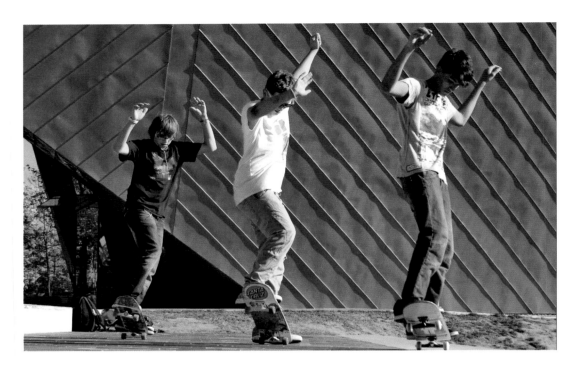

Skating

(*Above*) Three synchronised skateboarders practice their 'manuals' outside Firstsite, which rapidly became a popular venue for the sport. (*Below*) Three roller skaters zip around the rink at Rollerworld, one of Colchester's success stories down the years. *Photographs*: Michael Linton, Andrew Phillips.

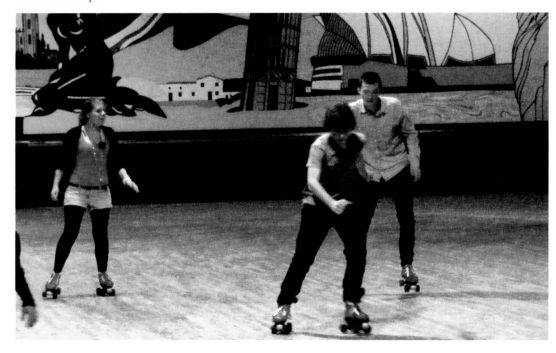

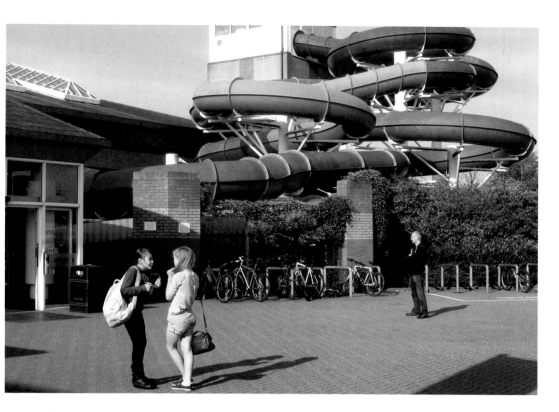

Swimming

With its imposing flumes snaking around its front, Colchester Leisure World (*above*) cuts an impressive figure on the town's landscape. As Colchester's largest sports complex it boasts a wealth of facilities, including multiple swimming pools, rapids, a wave machine, indoor sports centre, and Astroturf. (*Below*) A Saturday morning family swimming class at the Colchester Academy (former Sir Charles Lucas School). *Photographs*: Andrew Phillips, Anthony Roberts.

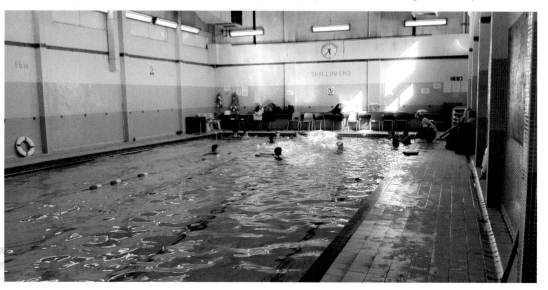

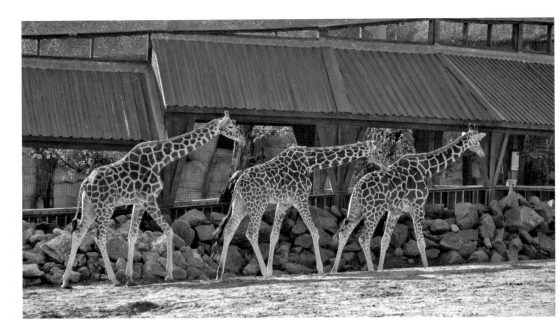

A Day Out

Colchester Zoo – winner of the 'Large Visitor Attraction of the Year' award – is the town's most visited tourist destination. It has had great success in breeding endangered species like white rhinos, red pandas and reticulated giraffes. (*Above*) Lili, Isha and Epesi, the zoo's first ever breeding group of giraffes, parade across the Edge of Africa enclosure. (*Below*) A group of young cub scouts walk through the Playa Patagonia, Europe's largest straight underwater tunnel. The subterranean walkway gives viewers the chance to see sea lions at close range. *Photographs*: Christine Alexander, Kate Jackson.

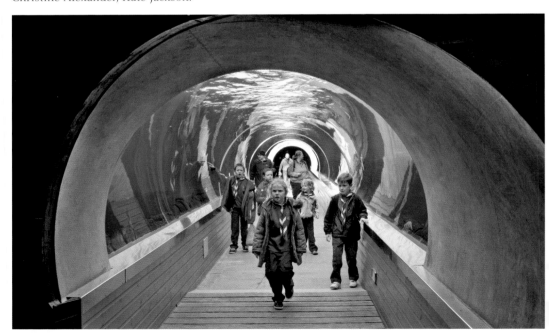

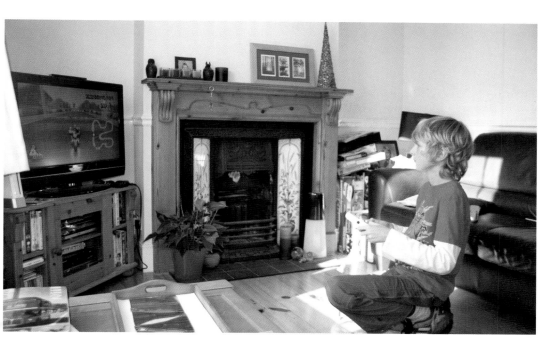

A Day In

(*Above*) In the comfort of his own home, ten-year-old Ben plays Mario Kart on his Nintendo Wii, a wireless games console that allows players to 'interact' with the screen. (*Below*) A Games Workshop in Colchester where people meet and paint figurines, as well as battle against each other in tabletop war games. *Photographs*: Cathy Constable, Richard Lyon.

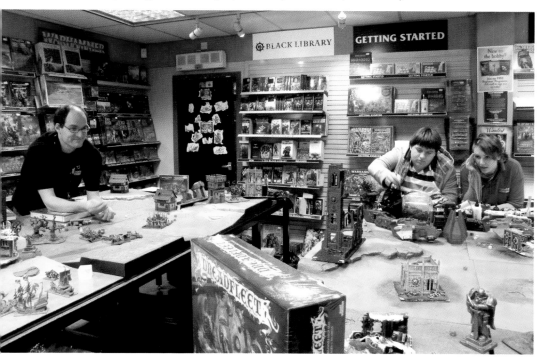

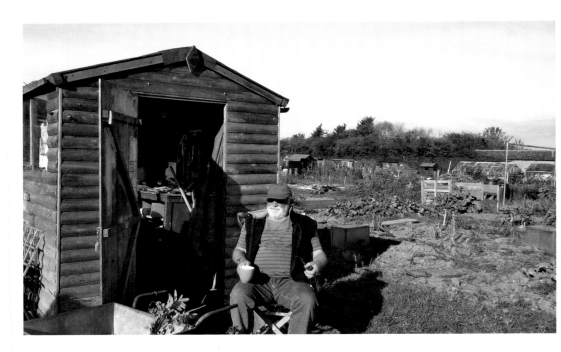

Green Fingers

Due to oversubscription, the council only allows one allotment per household, and newly-vacant plots are being halved to give more people the chance to experience 'allotmenteering' in nineteen sites across Colchester. John Bates (*above*) takes a tea break on his allotment, smoking his pipe, as becomes a former ship's captain. Lisa (*below*), a professional gardener, stands before the fruits of her labour: two bags of garden waste in specially provided, routinely collected, Borough Council bags. *Photographs*: Sandra Hartley, Andrew Phillips.

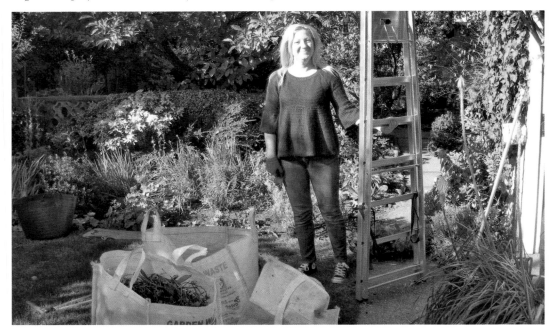

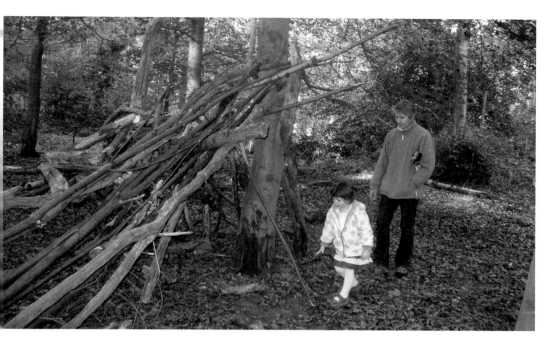

Green Colchester

(*Above*) Cristiane Mills takes her granddaughter, Elise, for a walk around High Woods Country Park, visiting one of several woodland dens found there. Thanks to the efforts of a handful of councillors, this area was saved in the 1980s from major housing development. (*Below*) Despite the apparently rural setting, these two fishermen are on Riverside Walk, a short distance from North Bridge. *Photographs*: Crystelle Mills Smith, John Lewell.

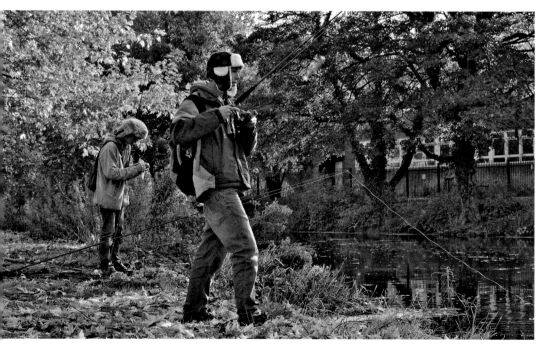

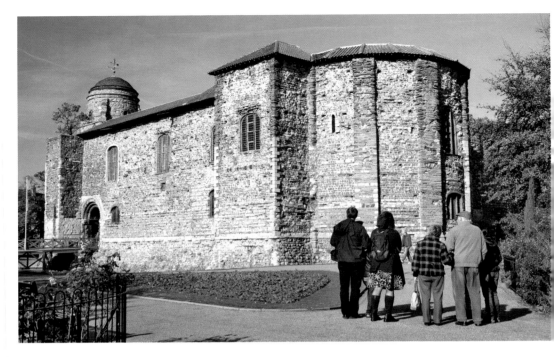

The Castle

(*Above*) William the Conqueror's castle guards one end of High Street. It is a 950-year-old building, built with 2,000-year-old Roman bricks. Today a cosier castle houses Colchester's flagship museum, surrounded by Colchester's award-winning Castle Park. Lower Castle Park is separated by a long section of the historic town wall (*below*), built after Colchester had been burnt to the ground by Boudicca. Today it provides a perfect pathway for dog walkers and joggers. *Photographs*: Stephanie Round, Nikki Hazelton.

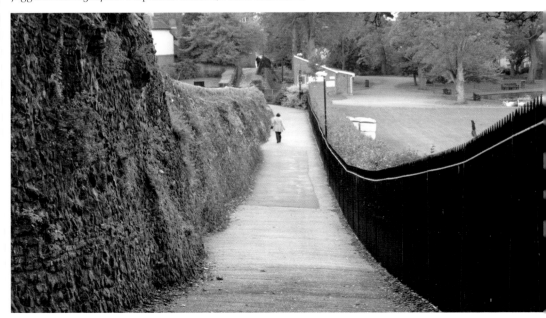

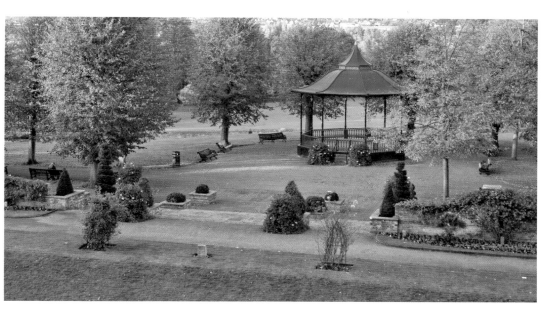

Castle Park

(*Above*) Behind the castle the ground falls dramatically away to Castle Park's original Victorian grandstand, now a listed building, where brass bands and orchestras still play. Autumnal colours create an idyllic scene less than 500 yards from Colchester's town centre. Beyond the bandstand the land falls faster still, past the Roman Wall and the Colchester & East Essex Cricket Club's ground to reach the River Colne, seen here (*below*) at its best. Stand still and wait – kingfishers visit here. *Photographs*: Lynda Robinson, Robert Fisher.

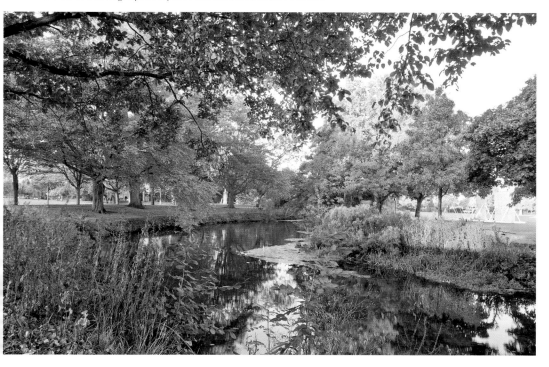

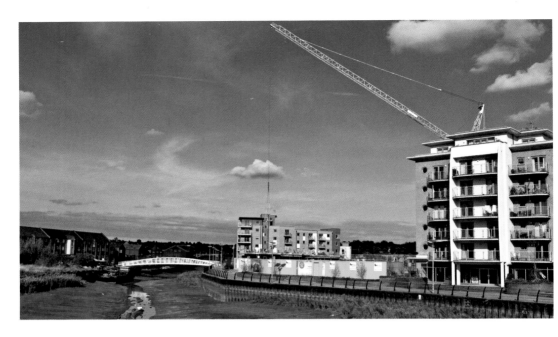

Tomorrow

This page is not the end. It is the beginning of the next twenty-five years; *Colchester 24* will return in 2036. Meanwhile Colchester will continue to grow, as it does at the 'new Hythe' (*above*). The town must also preserve its historic buildings. The Grosvenor Hotel (*below*) sits boarded up, but as a listed building it is protected. Other outstanding buildings are not. Colchester should now enforce its own 'Local List' of historic buildings. *Photographs*: Rodney Woods, Andrew Phillips.

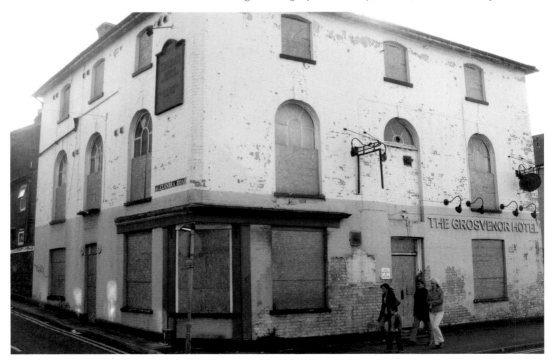